THE STRIKER AND THE CLOCK

THE STRIKER
AND THE CLOCK

On Being in the Game

GEORGIA CLOEPFIL

RIVERHEAD BOOKS   NEW YORK   2024

RIVERHEAD BOOKS
An imprint of Penguin Random House LLC
penguinrandomhouse.com

Earlier versions of portions of the book previously published in different form as:
"Beat the Clock" in *n+1* (July 2017); "Lucky to Be Here" in *Epiphany* (Fall/Winter 2020);
"Hungry" in *Sport Literate* (November 2020); "The Shape of a Dream Can Expand
and Shrink: An American Soccer Life in South Korea, Part I and II"
in *Howler* (August 2018).

LIBRARY OF CONGRESS CATALOGING-IN-PUBLICATION DATA
Names: Cloepfil, Georgia, author.
Title: The striker and the clock : on being in the game / Georgia Cloepfil.
Description: First hardcover edition. | New York, N.Y. : Riverhead Books, 2024.
Identifiers: LCCN 2023028935 (print) | LCCN 2023028936 (ebook) |
ISBN 9780593714881 (hardcover) | ISBN 9780593714904 (ebook)
Subjects: LCSH: Cloepfil, Georgia. | Women soccer players—
United States—Biography. | Women authors—United States—Biography.
Classification: LCC GV942.7.C557 A3 2024 (print) | LCC GV942.7.C557 (ebook) |
DDC 796.334092 [B]—dc23/eng/20230828
LC record available at https://lccn.loc.gov/2023028935
LC ebook record available at https://lccn.loc.gov/2023028936

Printed in the United States of America
1st Printing

Book design by Daniel Lagin

For Mom, Dad, and Cole

THE STRIKER AND THE CLOCK

1'

THE TEAM'S SPORTS PSYCHOLOGIST TOLD US, *THE EFFECTS OF visualization are most powerful if you incorporate every sense*. So, there I was on the bleachers before the game began: sweat smell, grass smell, mud smell, stretched leather hugging my feet, baggy polyester clinging to my damp skin. Every muscle tensed. When I closed my eyes, I could hear the sound of heavy breathing (mine) and directions being shouted from all sides (my teammates, my coaches).

The psychologist also mentioned that our vantage point was important, so I sat as close as I could to the center of the field and up high where I could see everything—even beyond the field, into the tall and sparse Swedish forests that bordered the stadium. Our home field in the small, central town of Karls-koga housed a collection of narrow, wooden benches and could accommodate about a hundred people. When there were more spectators at our games, they leaned against the half-made wooden fence that functioned as a barrier between the crowd and the players. From the top of the stands, I looked down on the still-empty field, all grass and mud and divots from the rainy spring. I got to work and watched myself in third person, just like in a dream.

Most days, I practiced visualizing in the shower. I visualized before going to bed, while eating cereal, while walking to the grocery store. It didn't take very long, and eventually, it didn't take much effort. Cue crowd noise. There might be light rain, slick grass. The wind was either hot or cold, depending on the forecast. I felt one foot planting in soft ground, while the other struck the ball with the laces of my cleat. I could hear the sound of the ball rolling down the net of the goal, *tick tick tick* against the strings, and landing on damp grass with a *thud*.

Of course, the task of visualization requires preparing for what you don't know, what you can't know, and what *might* happen. The game of soccer is fast-moving, organic, and unpredictable. There are no timeouts, and set plays only happen after fouls or corner kicks. Any number of combinations, passes, movements, and patterns might manifest while playing, and your job is to be ready even for what you can't possibly imagine.

Before each game, I watched this other Georgia in my mind as she broke through lines, ran down the wing, and shot the ball. I started again, projecting onto the green expanse of the field. This time, she backed toward the left sideline, received a pass, dribbled forward, and crossed the ball near the face of the goal, where a teammate stood to tap it in. This Georgia was full of confidence, happy, celebrating. Over and over, I tried to imagine her into a triumphant future.

The psychologist said it was important to go back and correct yourself if you happened to picture a missed shot, an injury, or a mistake of any kind. *The image you conjure should be perfect*, he said, *just as you would dream it to be.*

2'

I STILL HAVE DREAMS ABOUT SOCCER. SOME NIGHTS, I DREAM that I am playing on the national team, or on a men's professional team with Lionel Messi. Sometimes, I agree to go overseas again. I dream I have reentered the arc of my career. I revisit its origins on youth travel teams and in college in Minnesota. I am back in Australia for my first gig abroad. I dream I have moved on to play in Sweden, then to South Korea, Lithuania, or Norway. I dream I'm between contracts in Seattle, training alone on empty high school fields. I sometimes dream I've finally *made it*. I have dreams in which I am scoring beautiful goals.

In other dreams, I have forgotten something essential back at home: I put my cleats in the wrong bag; I got the time wrong, the field wrong, everything wrong. Most often, I have a dream in which I am trying to sprint across a field but I've lost the ability entirely. My legs feel leaden and stiff. My knees don't drive up with any amount of strength. I am trying my hardest, but it just won't work.

And sometimes my dreams about soccer are interrupted altogether. I wake up with a start, sweating, exhilarated, disoriented. Isn't this the worst feeling? Longing and curiosity color my morning, leak into the afternoon. I want to know how it ends.

3'

AT MY MOTHER'S HOUSE FOR THE HOLIDAYS, I SIFT THROUGH old diaries filled with notes I took when I was playing overseas. I find a DVD hidden in a messy box of old movies and video games in the attic of my childhood home. The plastic case has a sticker that reads: *Lincoln 1, Westview 0*. It is a recording of my high school State Championship game. I slip the disc into my old laptop and play it from the beginning. It takes me a moment to locate myself on the field. There—on the right wing.

On the screen, I look so small, quiet, like a stranger. Alienation is a close partner to observation. During my professional career, I thought of myself as confident and loud, a player who had a commanding presence on the field. I yelled at myself, at the referee, at my teammates. I fell with dramatic gestures, celebrated with aplomb, and marked my failures in any practice or game with complete devastation. But in this video, I'm still young, undeveloped as a player and a person. I am hugging the sidelines. This other Georgia doesn't gesture much with her hands. She doesn't demand the ball, doesn't take control of the game.

As I watch, I'm filled with a mysterious shame; the person in the video is me, but I don't feel like I can be held responsible for her decisions, for her style of play, or for the result of her efforts. So much has changed since then. I watch as she collides with a defender and falls to the turf. She gets up, but not quickly enough. She has lost the ball. I turn the video off before even five minutes have passed.

My own relationship to who I was feels tenuous. Is this true for everyone? I find I have no real memory of myself as a young player. I try to piece together a story of the day from the film, but my imagination fails me. I have so many questions for her. I ask them across time and get no reply: *What did you eat for breakfast? Who is your best friend? Do you feel loved? How much sleep are you getting?* I would like to know what she wore to school, if she drove or took the bus that day, if she was nervous or just excited about the game that evening. And I'd like to know what sort of plans she has for her future.

I try to extract individual scenes from an incomplete and flickering catalog of thousands of practices, games, and fields from my youth: I remember car rides and sunburns and slick rubber turf; putting my legs in the air so my mom could peel the stuck socks off of my rain-slicked calves; reaching a hand inside to pull them right side out and laying the socks on the heating vent until they hardened into stiff shells. I remember my dad playing the Who's "Won't Get Fooled Again" on the drive to a game; we'd wait for the final drum solo and then turn it up so loud my ears hurt. Once, I bit through my tongue playing goalie at recess, and I remember someone put a flower next to my arm as I bent into the nurse's sink, bleeding. By the time I turned around, they were gone.

If we are lucky, when we are young, we get to feel the full sense of our own potential. We are all possibility. Nothing has happened to us yet, so anything might. The people we knew back then are special to us because they will always remind us of a time before our life happened. I'm not in touch with most of the teammates I grew up playing with; I haven't talked to anyone from my high school team in more than ten years. But still, my memories of life's big events circle around soccer. The sport was my witness. I try not to stray too far from it, so I can remain in touch with all the versions of myself that it conjures.

4'

DURING THE SPRING SEMESTER OF MY SENIOR YEAR IN COL-
lege, a teammate drove with me to a professional tryout in
Chicago. We stayed in the suburban home of another friend's
parents and, in the morning, drove on salt-stained highways to
an indoor soccer warehouse. Inside, there were close to a hundred other women leaning against the plexiglass walls that surrounded the field. They laced up their cleats, scrolled nervously
on their phones, and tied their hair back into tight ponytails.
Eventually, the coach gathered us in the middle of the field, and
I looked down at all of our feet. Against the flawless AstroTurf,
our shoes were a clashing mix of metallic and neon colors, leather
and plastic. Nike Hypervenoms, brand-new Adidas Nemeziz
and Copas, Puma Kings. Mine were Nike Vapors; I'd worn the
same style since I was in the third grade. I had a silver-and-blue
pair when I joined the boys' football team, and navy and black
the year I quit. I had a white-orange-and-blue pair all throughout college and black ones with a neon-orange lining when I
signed my first professional contract. They are expensive shoes;

the best new cleats cost around $200. The design doesn't change much, but the shoes get lighter and lighter each year, shedding ounces until they weigh no more than a sock. At the tryout, I could tell who had invested recently and who was wearing shoes from years ago, perhaps for the first time in a while. I was invited back for a second day of tryouts before I was cut. On the drive back to Minnesota, I wondered silently when I would be able to justify buying myself a new pair.

5'

VISUALIZATION IS AN ACT OF REVISION. IT TAKES PLACE BE-
fore the final performance, when there is still time to go back,
to reimagine, to erase or to repeat. When I write, I am endowed
with this same control. I can delete, I can move things around,
I can keep it all to myself if I prefer. But once the game starts,
soccer is all forward motion. Time on the clock progresses
steadily from 0 to 90 minutes. Everything that happens is confined to the clock's predetermined boundary, a temporal perimeter of an hour and a half. There are no stoppages, no timeouts,
no pauses except for a break at halftime. The waning clock is
animate: it is a foe if more time is needed, a friend if it's best
for the game to end. Like the clock, a striker's body moves
compulsively forward. We aim to travel from the defensive end
of the field to the attack. We orient ourselves toward a goal.

There's an element of propulsion in the name of the position I played: striker or *forward*. The forward plays farthest up
the field and is, therefore, the one with most responsibility for
scoring or creating goals. A striker's movements make space for

the attack, push against the boundary of an opponent's defensive line. In the old English sense, forward means *of the future*.

Tactically, each position in soccer is represented not only by a name but also a number. Ten for the attacking center midfielder, four for the central defender, nine for the central striker. The numbers are representative of a player's role on the team and their place in the formation; a six is a reliable link between defense and midfield, an eleven is a speedy showboat on the wing. Some coaches prefer when a player is versatile. It's good to have someone on a team who can fill different roles, someone who has avoided being flattened by the duty of perfecting a single position. But the more I played, the more I saw myself solidly as an outside forward. I hardened into a rigid and inflexible *seven*. My heels sought the chalky white of the sideline. I liked when the whole field was in front of me.

So, when I was given an option, the number I picked for my jersey was the same as the one that represented my best position. Seven is a prime number. Seven is a lucky number. Seven means the creation of all things. In Pythagorean numerology, the number seven represents the union of the physical world (four) with the spiritual (three). There are seven oceans, seven continents, seven vertebrae in your neck.

6'

ON THE FIELD, A STRIKER IS COACHED TO FORGET. ONLY BY doing so can we be carried forward by the power of this forgetting. We should forget missed shots, poorly timed runs, touches on the ball that betray us and fall out of reach. This way, we can be completely present on the field. We can be ready for what might come next and avoid dwelling on past mistakes. We must move past our errors during a game, maintain composure, and play on.

A forward's opportunities to score in a game are few, if any. Coaches and analysts describe scoring as the most difficult thing to accomplish in soccer. A single goal might be the difference between winning and losing, a single mistake likewise. In some ways, it's easy to dissect a holistic team effort into individual triumphs and failures. Each pass, trap, save, or shot is directly connected to what came before it or what will come after. But errors and achievements can also be isolated and assessed. I held on to my mistakes and replayed bad decisions. After games, I watched video and picked apart my play. I hung my head on the field after a poor shot, berated myself, cursed and yelled at no one in particular.

The impulse of an athlete toward meticulous self-improvement, and perhaps that of a writer to document, runs up against the coach's instruction to have a short memory. As a player, I struggled with this important skill.

7'

THE PENALTY KICK IS THE MOST ISOLATED OF ALL SCORING opportunities. In some ways, it is the easiest: a free shot on goal, no defenders, all stillness. But the pressure is immense. During a penalty kick, there is no way to hide in the movement and exchange of bodies or the speed of play. The whistle blows, the game pauses. All eyes are on the striker and the goalkeeper. I took only a handful of these shots throughout my career, and I can still remember, with great detail, the three I missed:

2015: SWEDEN, DIVISION 2, LEAGUE GAME. My dad and step-mom had flown over from the US to watch. I was the leading scorer on my team, averaging more than a goal per game. I was feeling confident. So, when I was fouled in the box, I didn't hesitate before stepping up to take the kick. I tried to chip the ball over the keeper, an act of out-of-character bravado, and it soared over the crossbar.

2013: MINNESOTA, COLLEGE, CONFERENCE TOURNAMENT FINAL.
A teammate was fouled in the box with the game tied, 0–0. I
took the penalty kick, and the keeper made a good save on an
okay shot. Our defensive effort was paralyzed by my error, the
team frozen by surprise and disappointment. Our opponent
scored almost immediately on a counterattack. I still feel responsible for the final score. The entire game unfolded around
my missed shot.

2009: PORTLAND, HIGH SCHOOL, STATE SEMIFINAL TOURNA-
MENT. I was the second person to take a penalty in the shoot-
out. I struck the ball poorly, driving it to the middle-right, and
the keeper made an easy save. Our team went on to win, and
the photo in the local paper the next morning showed me
screaming with enormous, animal relief atop of a pile of celebrating teammates. At school the next day, my English teacher
handed back an essay with a note at the bottom of the final page:
a girl who can write like this ought not worry about goal-kicks.

8'

ONCE, BETWEEN PROFESSIONAL SEASONS, I DROVE WITH MY
family to an amusement park. My eight-year-old sibling was
most excited for the roller coaster, which they were finally tall
enough to ride. They surveyed the passengers in the car, asked
us all, *What do you think is the best feeling in the world?* Without
hesitating or letting anyone else answer first, I told them: *Scoring a goal.* But I had a hard time explaining why. I thought it
might have something to do with the feeling of pure accomplishment, the praise, or the embrace of teammates. And then
there are the hormones, the physical response to elation.

Authors I adore write about the ways pain eludes language.
In *The Body in Pain*, Elaine Scarry writes: *Physical pain does not
simply resist language but actively destroys it.* In *On Illness*, Virginia Woolf writes: *let a sufferer try to describe a pain in his head
to a doctor and language at once runs dry.* But I can't remember
reading as much about the difficulties one faces when attempt-
ing to transcribe pure delight, blacked-out bliss, euphoria.

Like the span of a career, the narrative of a single game is

17

full of empty space and irretrievable moments. I have particular difficulty recalling the precise joy of scoring a goal, the actual memory of which, I've read, can be erased by the surge of adrenaline. In her memoir, *Forward*, Abby Wambach writes of this feeling: *as soon as leather met rope the picture went black—not a slow fade, but a swift guillotine chop that separated the scene from my ability to see it*. I can only approximate. I can only think backward and imagine. As with the rest of life, it's difficult to distinguish between my own memories of scoring and what I have seen re-created in photos or videos. So, I remember each of my goals from the perspective of a camera. Sometimes I worry that the gaps in my recollection disqualify me from being able to write honestly about my experiences playing.

I look to others to help me understand this feeling that I know so well in my body. I read interviews with famous goalscorers and watch documentaries about illustrious soccer careers. A reporter once asked Wayne Rooney, the famous English striker, to explain what it felt like to score a goal in the English Premier League, and he said, *the initial feeling, it's like you're playing football under water*. This image, almost otherworldly, fantastical, is the closest approximation I've encountered. Rooney went on to give some context for this remark: the moment after scoring feels like coming up for air, he explained. Suddenly, you can sense the atmosphere above the surface. You can hear the fans, your teammates, the coaches. Muted focus gives way to vibrant and complete sensation. It is eerily quiet under water, even your own mind can fall silent, separated from the demands and distractions of the world above the surface. Once again, the idea that there is an above and a below, a guillotine, a break, a threshold of wordlessness. And once again, I worry this severance is such an integral part of the experience that, each time I go to write about the joy of playing, I must be making it up.

9'

I SCORED MY FIRST PROFESSIONAL GOAL ON A LATE SUMMER day in the Melbourne suburbs. I had carpooled to the field with a girl who lived just down the road from me. Our team was playing in a preseason tournament in February, and our uniforms weren't printed yet, so we wore neon-green practice shirts and navy shorts. I had tape on my knee, because a not-so-distant operation made the joint ache subtly around the surgery's scars. As is the case with most exhibitions, this game was not filmed, so I tend to think my memory of it is authentic. I hold it close now. In the second half, the ball was played out to my teammate Melina, who dribbled to the end line. I ran to keep up with her, and she crossed the ball to me for an easy finish into the goal. Right place, right time. We won the game 1–0. As with my other goals, when I think of it now, I see the moment play out from above. It's as though time and distance have pulled me out of and away from my body. I remember nothing of the emotion except a feeling of validation: this was why I was there.

10'

AS A CHILD, I WANTED TO BE GOOD MORE THAN ANYTHING. Often, I specifically wanted to be *better than Hannah and Adriane*, my older sisters, who played soccer through middle school and high school. Our parents supported each of us in sports, just as they did in any hobby. And they held a healthy urban skepticism toward the intensity of youth travel soccer (the expense, the pressure, the showcases, and the college commitments from thirteen-year-olds). My mother had been a state champion sprinter on her track team in high school and ran for a year at the University of Oregon. My father had captained his perpetually winless high school football team. They paid, they drove, they encouraged, and they loved watching us play. But when the coach of my under-ten team suggested they should put me on a boys team, my parents were amused and perplexed. I imagine they rolled their eyes. I was playing with all of my friends. I was doing just fine.

In childhood, there were only so many places I could exert

control. The goodness I was after could be cultivated in the classroom, at the dinner table, or while playing in the neighborhood. Straight A's, a role in the musical, a gold medal at the track meet . . . always, I felt the most validated on the soccer field. I was a dog running after a stick; I was rewarded and beloved for my tricks. On the field, life became very small, contained by the shape of a rectangle and held close by straight, white lines painted with chalk.

A teammate once lent me the book *Flow*. In it, psychologist Mihaly Csikszentmihalyi presents the concept of a *flow state* to describe the achievement of optimal experience or deep concentration and enjoyment. Flow is most often associated with creativity and athletics. *What makes [sports] conducive to flow*, Csikszentmihalyi writes, *is that they were* designed *to make optimal experience easier to achieve. They have rules that require the learning of skills, they set up goals, they provide feedback, they make control possible.* A game is designed, in other words, to facilitate a world in which clarity of value reigns. There is no ambiguity here. The player exists in a liminal space between success and failure—in a constant state of striving—and knows precisely in which direction they are headed.

It's no surprise to me that many former athletes end up in the corporate world, where, I imagine, their boss rewards them, they are part of a good team, they get promoted, they are rated and reviewed. Even years after playing my last professional soccer game, I still long for the game's clear sense of accomplishment. I am no longer privileged by the consistent and productive feedback. Only on the field was achievement so ordered and simple, failure and success so distinct, their results so obvious and public. While playing, I didn't have to think about what mattered. The constraints, the limitations of the game, produced freedom.

11'

AS I WRITE THIS, I'M REREADING VIRGINIA WOOLF'S *THE WAVES*. It is one of the five books that traveled with me everywhere I played. The book's edges have been rounded by wear; the binding barely holds the book together. As always, my attention is drawn to Percival, a minor character in the book. He is portrayed as a simpleton who plays sports in the schoolyard and rides a horse into war, unthinking. We never hear his point of view; instead, we learn about Percival from the various voices who narrate the book. Neville describes him with erotic love and infatuation: *Not a thread, not a sheet of paper lies between him and the sun, between him and the rain, between him and the moon as he lies naked, tumbled, hot, on his bed.* Percival's relationship to his body is wholesome. The attention he attracts has to do with his closeness to the physical elements of existence and his implied lack of intellect. Percival is saintly. He is adored and, to some degree, envied by those who observe him for his stupidity, for the contentment apparent in his one-dimensional prayers. *And he will pray,* Neville imagines, *"Lord let us win." He will think of one thing only.*

I like to think of Percival as a striker, his mind empty as the ball crosses the goal line.

12'

I PASSED SOME FALL EVENINGS AFTER COLLEGE WATCHING MY
boyfriend Cole play at the stadium a couple of blocks away from
where I lived. He was still in school the year after I graduated,
and I'd stayed in Minneapolis to keep my job at the local bookstore while I figured out what to do next. On those nights, I
sat alone, hiding near the top of the stands, and soccer rested
at the pit of my stomach. It was tarry blackness. It was heavy
and difficult; it wouldn't leave. I felt an ambient shame but had
no object for my disappointment. I hid in an oversize hoodie
as I watched. In my nebulous young adulthood, I longed for the
comfort and confidence soccer had brought me. I felt like I
should still be out there on the field. I couldn't recognize that
my grief was private—no one else could see it.

Cole liked to remind me of an NCAA commercial: a pho-
tomontage of young adults in lab coats, at long meeting tables,
on farms. *Ninety-eight percent of college athletes will go pro in
something other than sports*, it said. He meant: it will work out
either way.

He was the first boy I loved who also loved soccer, and sometimes I think he helped me enjoy the game in a way boyfriends before him had not. With Cole, I was uninhibited; I could be dumb and buoyant, could care only about the ball. And I think soccer helped me love him back. Soccer was a reminder of what it meant to pursue joy above anything else.

Cole was vocal, strong, and successful. When we embraced after his game, the familiar scent of effort rubbed off on me. I clung to it, breathed in deeply.

13'

THE LIFE OF A WOMAN SOCCER PLAYER IS SCATTERED AND OB-
scure, a private endeavor experienced by only a handful of people
at a time. Most of us weren't on a national team, and cable-TV
cameras were rare—so rare they didn't usually appear at all.
Unlike most men's sports, there was no database for women's
stats. With limited media coverage, it was difficult to find
meaningful information about individuals or teams or agents.

In 2013, when I was a junior in college, the National Women's
Soccer League was established. It was the third iteration of an
American professional league. The NWSL still exists now and
has become the longest-running women's soccer league in the
history of the country. When I trialed for the team in Chicago as
a senior, only one Division III college soccer player like me had
ever taken the field for one of the eight professional teams; opportunities and exposure at that level were particularly limited.

After college ended, I spent much of my time googling
women's soccer agents, *women's professional soccer*, *how to get a job
playing overseas*. I emailed every coach I'd had in the past ten

years. Garrett, Lauren, Michelle, Jemma. I emailed all of the people they told me to email. I sent missives onto the internet and hoped I might contact someone who would be able to help me keep playing. A couple of people got back to me; most didn't. I had coffee with the friend of a friend who gave me the email of an agent she really couldn't recommend; he was just the only one she knew. I fantasized about doing a service for the women's game by streamlining all of this information on a website. The agent didn't respond.

In order to get a job, a player has to sign a contract during either the summer or winter transfer window. Opportunities come and go during these month-long periods as teams build their rosters. It is the same with all sports, but the sense of scarcity that pervades the women's professional landscape adds a certain amount of desperation and urgency to the process. You had to be ready to say yes.

One year, an agent called while I was sitting on my bed at home. One year, an agent called while I was at my temp job. An agent called while I was grocery shopping with my mom, while I was on a walk with Cole. An agent left a voicemail: *please call me back as soon as possible.* Another emailed: *WhatsApp. Urgent.* Often the window of time between signing a contract and leaving the country was just a couple of days. Hesitate, and it would close.

I spent hours at my day jobs googling unfamiliar cities as offers surfaced and then disappeared. I scoured the suburbs of Seville on satellite view, examined the roofs of buildings in

Gothenburg. I eyed a long, sandy beach interrupted by piers and development on the edges of Lisbon. I studied public transit maps and tourist websites, trying to imagine myself into a new life.

Often the opportunity came at someone else's expense. When I was offered a contract to play in Korea, it was to replace a player who'd fractured her pelvic bone. In Norway, I took the place of a girl who'd torn her ACL and had to miss half of the season. Her name was Freja. After I had been in Norway for only a week, we went on a long hike together; she hadn't had surgery yet. When we got to the peak, she talked to me about the medical decisions that lay ahead of her, the implications they might have on her career. We sat on a rock overlooking Arna, the suburb of Bergen where we lived. As we rested, she massaged her knee. The village was green and compact and mingled with pockets of ocean. Fishing boats docked and unloaded their yield. Norway was the most beautiful place I'd ever been. Finally, Freja said what we both knew: *if I hadn't gotten hurt, you wouldn't be here.*

It was seven months after graduating college when I signed my first contract with a semipro team in Australia. The opportunity felt like a lifeline. One day after my phone call with the team's manager, I packed everything I owned into my Saab, strapped my mattress to the roof, parked the car in a rented garage, and got on a plane. The offer (a one-year contract) felt like a thing that would never happen again, which, though I couldn't know it yet, was how it would always feel. I wrote it at the start of emails to coaches, agents, friends, my parents. I practiced saying it to myself: *I feel so lucky to have this opportunity.*

14'

EACH TIME I LANDED, THERE WOULD BE SOMEONE WAITING for me at the airport. He would be wearing a suit, looking for someone tall, someone blond. He might have seen a photo of me, or he might have just been guessing. He would be right, though, and he would approach me with a tentative smile, which I would return. I would notice the crest on his polo or sport coat. *Georgia?!* We would shake hands. He would offer to hold my bags, but I wouldn't give them away. *I am fine. I am strong. I am not tired.* But really, the jet lag was fatiguing already, as my flight would not have been direct, nor first class. I would have spent the night before in tears of excitement and sadness. I would have said goodbye to my family; Cole would have dropped me off at the airport at an ungodly hour. I would have packed everything I needed into one suitcase, because I was perpetually afraid of overpacking. I was good at traveling light. I would know exactly what I needed for a single year in any country, and I would bring with me nothing more than that. The man at the airport was the manager or the agent. He would be excited to have me there. He might have offered me food, *you must be hungry*, and watched as I self-consciously nibbled at a salad or a snack or a sandwich. I was consumed with the need to appear self-contained, to seem like a person who could confront the unknown without fear or hesitation. On the flight over, I would have prepared myself for any living situation, for any working environment. I had signed a contract, so I knew I needed to last the year, and I could do that no matter what. When I got to the house, the dorm, the apartment, I would want nothing more than to close the door, lie back on the bed, and exhale. I could do this for one minute, but then I would be ushered to training, to the office, to sign papers, get a visa, make a bank account. Life was beginning again, this time: here.

15'

AFTER FIFTEEN MINUTES HAVE PASSED, TIME IS ABUNDANT.
The beginning of the game, like the beginning of a life, is
bloated with possibility. We are acquainting ourselves with our
opponent, each of us is testing our mark. How fast are they?
How do they move across the field? Which foot do they prefer?
We search for the opportunity to assert our special abilities in
the smallest of spaces.

We begin the game just as the sun sets, so the stadium lights
are turned on in anticipation of darkness. Their bulbs slowly
warm until a circle of brightness envelops the field. Light comes
from each corner, and a player is ringed by silhouettes of her
own body. A four-pointed star of shadows casts out from where
her feet meet the ground.

After fifteen minutes have passed, the nerves settle. Space
opens up. The ball calms down. The game finds a rhythm and
a personality unique to the conditions of this particular day. It
will continue like this for some time.

16'

NO MATTER HOW MUCH TIME PASSED BETWEEN CONTRACTS, games, seasons, every detail of the pregame ritual remained familiar, its contours vivid and particular. Every locker room was the same; each girl had a cage for her gear and a plaque with her name on it at the top. Each room had the same smell, too: a mix of grass and sweat, of very fresh air and the stench of partly rotting cleats.

In Melbourne, our team played at a public park where the field shared a space with a dog park, a playground, and a cricket pitch. The field where we trained and played was in the suburb of Ashburton, three train stops from where I lived. Our season ran from February to September, through the winter in Australia. During one of my first games, I noticed a bed of dried eucalyptus leaves beneath my feet. When I looked up, the sunset was obscured by these strange, spindly trees, the air scented with them.

Our locker room was a row of benches with hooks at head

level. Before each game, Rebecca sat and put on her socks before she did anything else: the right, then the left. I remember another teammate, Melissa, who danced in the middle of the room and played music on a portable speaker. The first song on her list was Eminem's "Lose Yourself," and everyone agreed the song had had its day. Emma, or maybe it was Maria, had a long list of things she needed to do before games—small tasks that didn't take much time. A purple headband, tape on her right wrist, a short prayer, her hair pulled into a tight, neat bun like a ballerina. Scout also did her hair, tied it in two French braids. The team had won every game since she started wearing it like that.

Nerves are good, everyone said. They make you alert; they mean you care; they feel like a low hum. Nerves were all anticipation, no fear. They were simply a part of my preparation; my body willfully conjured their busy vibrations. I listened to music before games and paced the hallways outside of the locker room. I liked to have a moment to myself. I performed seriousness this way, hoping it would invoke actual intensity and focus. I practiced visualization while the playlist I'd made in college pulsed through noise-cancelling headphones—the familiarity of the old songs felt like an important part of the ritual.

17'

OVER TIME, I BECAME WELL PRACTICED IN THE ART OF *ALMOST* being somewhere. I was skilled at establishing a home in a short amount of time. I unpacked in a hurry when I arrived in a new country. Repeated iteration becomes habit, and habit becomes custom. The rentals in which we were housed were always sparsely furnished. There was always an IKEA table and rug, a TV, a coffee maker. There was always a bike, sometimes a car, never enough money for gas. There was always a roommate, usually another American, to whom I grew close and from whom I fell away when I moved again. I came to know the few things that made me feel more at home and, even if I was only going to live there for three months, I sought them out in my first week: a vase for flowers, a down comforter for my bed, a painting to hang on my wall. When I left home, I packed my suitcase with two bags of Peet's ground coffee, five paperback books, and three photographs: Pacific Ocean, boyfriend, façade of childhood home. The objects were a map of myself; when I looked at them, I could see every place I'd ever lived, no matter how temporary or precarious.

In Australia, I rented a shotgun house with a roommate from Sydney who cooked dinner for me and encouraged me to smash plates on the back patio when I was upset. In Lithuania, I had a room to myself in a three-bedroom apartment, where I lived with two teammates above an older couple who always offered us coffee and, sometimes, a shot of sweet, honeyed krupnikas before our games. In Sweden, I shared a two-bedroom with the other American. We played soccer with the refugees who lived in the same housing development, and they showed us where to pick blueberries on the floor of the surrounding forest. In Korea, I lived in a dorm compound which was two stops away from the airport by train. In my free time, I rode back and walked in circles around the concourse.

We were always packing and unpacking. Sometimes we had three games in a week, each in a different corner of the country. We were given standard-issue suitcases with our number written in Sharpie in the top corner. When one teammate saw my clothes and uniforms thrown in my carry-on with messy haste, she promised to sit me down and make me learn *the Korean way* of folding clothes (each shirt folded in half, sleeves tucked inside themselves like a pocket. In the end, you could throw the parceled clothing across the room, and it would remain in its shape). In her drawers were rows of shirts and shorts, each in a compact square. When we traveled, her suitcase looked almost empty.

18'

SOMETIMES I ASSOCIATED ARRIVAL WITH MOVEMENT; I WAS committed to the belief that things in motion were better than things at rest. A friend of mine played in Germany for ten years. She fell in love there, had a job, a community of friends, and a new language. When she asks me why I moved around so much, why I didn't stay on a team longer than a year, I can only think it is because the movement was forgiving. There was always a reason to leave, and it was different every time. I wanted to be on a better team, I wasn't happy off the field, I wanted to play at a higher level, I wanted to live in a different city. Each change meant the prospect of beginning again. The specter of disappointment and failure, of *not making it* or never arriving, was softened by the physical range of my achievements; in the end I played in six countries, on four different continents: Australia, Sweden, Korea, Lithuania, United States, Norway.

In graduate school for a masters in creative writing, I was assigned to read *The Anatomy of Harpo Marx* by Wayne Koestenbaum. The book analyzes each gesture of the silent actor in the Marx Brothers' movies. Here he blows a bubble, here he is embraced, here is his face in profile. I was drawn to the monomania of this project. I love to read books by writers who are dogged by a singular pursuit, infatuated with the act of following. Of his own obsession that shapes the book's focus on a single character, Koestenbaum writes, *Why do I want more? Why do I love the process of wanting more more than I want the "more" itself?*

I still haven't managed to rid myself of the impulse toward movement. Even in a job I love, I look for others in nearby cities. Settling into a new home, I browse the rental listings compulsively; I still think of my future as something which is moving away from me, and I can't help but prepare to chase it.

19'

IN TIBETAN BUDDHISM, HUNGRY GHOSTS DWELL IN THEIR OWN realm on the Wheel of Life. They are teardrop shaped and have necks so thin that to eat would be painful, to swallow impossible. Their mouths are the size of a needle's eye, and they have stomachs as vast as a mountain. These ghosts are representative of souls who, even in the afterlife, are saddled with terrestrial, material desires. They want more.

Before games in Korea, I was allowed to request whatever food I wanted. Every week, I ordered grilled steak, greens, omelets, rice with kimchi, and soybeans. We ate three hours before the game, and I stayed at the table long after my teammates excused themselves. I finished off every bowl of banchan, every grain of rice. When we needed extra, they sent boxes of fried chicken to our rooms late at night, and we sat in circles on the floor eating until it was gone.

In our limited free time, we walked to 7-Eleven to buy snacks and eat instant ramen at the counter. I liked these daily excursions. They passed the time. The convenience stores had the comforts and the fluorescence of home. The snacks were much the same—Pringles, Kit Kat, Coca-Cola. But everything had a different flavor: green-tea and cherry-blossom chocolate, lychee soda. I learned to say yes to all food as I had learned to say yes to contract stipulations, flight times, and living arrangements. When my new friend held out a Dixie cup full of boiled chrysalises, I skewered a bug with a toothpick and crunched into its liquid-filled shell. The mineral taste of soil filled my mouth.

When we played well, the head coach treated us to barbecued eel or intestines. When we played poorly, he watched while we ran laps around the nearly concrete playing field, pounding our legs and backs into submission on the ancient turf. We played poorly enough, for long enough, that I developed a bulging disc in my back that still bothers me now. I could feel it swell and resonate with each step, but I couldn't stop running.

Often, international players were fed two meals a day at the team's clubhouse or at various restaurants whose sponsorship involved giving us free food. At a certain point each season, when I was sick of eating out, I'd make it a challenge to cook familiar recipes from unfamiliar grocery store offerings. It was impossible to find pure butter for chocolate chip cookies in Sweden. I couldn't source natural peanut butter in Korea or maple syrup in Norway. In Lithuania, I often went on an evening walk to the grocery store on the corner of our block where I filled a basket with carrots, potatoes, and beets for less than five dollars. When I walked home, I could see our Ukrainian teammates, who lived on the third floor, leaning out their window and smoking cigarettes. I waved before unlocking the front door.

20'

THE SOCCER LANDSCAPE OF MY CHILDHOOD WAS DOTTED WITH fast food and truck-stop dinners. Sub sandwiches and spaghetti. Piles of damp pizza boxes in the aisle of the bus, liters of soda poured into open mouths. The food we were fed was sustenance. It wasn't meant to taste good, to be savored or enjoyed. There is a thirty-minute window directly after exercise in which you must refuel the body if you want it to recover properly.

My family always told me I ate like a growing boy. But I stopped growing when I was fourteen. I wonder where all of the extra went. I think about how a body uses time and energy, how it burns itself up. At my hungriest, I would finish an entire entrée of ravioli before my family had been served their meal and then order another plate to eat with them. Other times, I barely skimmed the top of the salad bar offerings: shaved beets, spinach, sunflower seeds. My hunger grew and shrank with the size of my ambition.

During the 2008 Summer Olympics, swimmer Michael Phelps documented his daily food intake for a reporter at the

New York Post. Breakfast: three fried-egg sandwiches, coffee, a
five-egg omelet, a bowl of grits, three slices of French toast,
three chocolate-chip pancakes. Lunch: one pound of pasta, two
large ham and cheese sandwiches, energy drinks. Dinner: one
pound of pasta, an entire pizza, more energy drinks. Some elite
athletes have to consume nearly 8,000 calories to break even.

My number was closer to 4,000, but eating so much still
drove me crazy. Often, by the time I finished a meal, I was
already thinking about the next. I ate toast and ice cream just
to pad the numbers. I got full before I had eaten enough, so I
ate six times a day.

At practice, we wore tracking devices that told us how many
calories we burned, how fast we ran, and how much distance
we covered. I obsessed over my stats. I found myself motivated
by their concrete and calculated feedback. The average practice: 1,500 calories, 30.1 kmh, 6.1 miles.

21'

IN COLLEGE, THE FOOTBALL PLAYERS AT OUR SCHOOL WERE instructed by nutritionists and coaches to eat multiple burgers at both lunch and dinner. They gorged themselves to gain weight, to bulk up, to obey their coach, to be better at their sport. They gathered around the dining-hall bar tops and ate straight through an hour-long meal. In the spring, after the seniors had suited up for their final game, I noticed this was one of the last of their habits to die. I still remember the image of the graduating men swiveling on barstools at the grill counter wondering when they should stop, mindlessly squirting ketchup onto their patties.

A former teammate mused about her retirement in a blog; she claimed it was only after she quit that she began to recognize the low level of stress she'd grown accustomed to living with. The feeling manifested as a chorus of questions which accompanied her throughout each day. What if I walk there instead of drive? What if I have a glass of wine with dinner? What if I eat only two hours before the game? What if I have an apple instead of a banana? What if I eat too close to bed-time? What if I don't sleep enough? What if I agree to see this friend the night before a difficult practice? The echoes of these questions reverberated long past their relevance.

It hadn't occurred to me that I would need to reacquaint myself with the basic needs of my body after I stopped playing. Its demands would change and take up a different amount of space inside my mind.

22'

THE PHRASE *ARRIVAL FALLACY* IS USED TO DESCRIBE THE IL-lusion that, once you have accomplished a goal, arrived at its landmark, you will feel satisfied or at peace with where you are; you will stop desiring. What really happens is you become adjusted to your new state of being, and a fresh disappointment creeps in. The equation is exponential; when the destination recalibrates, it is always farther away.

I think of the hungry ghosts milling about on the edges of both life and death. Their realm is just above hell and just below human. Some ghosts can never reach what they desire. They are thirsty, and the mirage of a faraway stream torments them.

A striker, when they are playing with particular ferocity, is sometimes described as *hungry* for goals. It is important for her to stay hungry, always desirous. I have come to understand that my own infinite appetite was a fuel for my success. I am grateful to it and, for this reason, have a difficult time letting go. I find it hard to distinguish between wanting, the idea of wanting, and the habit of wanting. I am still unsure: is there an end point? Not a point at which one has played the best soccer, but at which one has played *enough*?

My hunger was and remains an exhausting burden. I am still practicing how to move less, how to feel fullness. *Someday,* my mother once told me with a laugh, *you won't be able to eat like this.*

23'

EMILY HAD A LOGICAL REASON FOR CONTINUING TO PLAY. SOC-
cer paid for her college and then supported her travels to new
countries. She often mentioned going out on a high note. Jen
embraced the slow decline. When she was younger, she'd been
a defender in the top league (my teammate tells me she was a
brutal opponent), but she was sliding down the ranks, stepping
away slowly. She played in a fifth-tier league. She had children
and talked about a future in coaching. Robyn played because
she still wanted to get better, maybe to be the best. She was a
skilled athlete who knew she was special. But she was also
running against the clock. She was twenty-five and had the
dreams of a fourteen-year-old. Hannah was four when she
started playing. Her parents attended every one of her games.
Fear kept Hannah going. *I don't know what I would do without
football*, she told me once as we made flower crowns for a mid-
summer celebration with her family. She wore a tight blond
ponytail, and baby hairs swirled in a halo that framed her face.
I prayed she wouldn't get injured and was careful never to

mention that someday she, too, would be too old. But not yet. She was only seventeen.

My soccer dream was shapeshifting. It was elusive and tricky. It moved forward tentatively, stepping around folding leagues and relegated teams. It pivoted away from coaches with bad reputations and limited roster numbers. It expanded to fill the contours of new opportunities for women, new paid leagues in Europe, more teams in the United States.

Women couldn't play soccer professionally in the United States until 2001, when the Women's United Soccer Association (WUSA) began play. The league ran for three full seasons and suspended operations on September 15, 2003, due to financial problems and the oft-cited *lack of public interest in the sport*. During my junior year of high school, Women's Professional Soccer (WPS) was launched. This league also folded after just three years. The NWSL was established in 2012 and, as I write this, is gearing up for its eleventh season.

I followed my dreams tirelessly. I wanted to improve, I wanted to win; above all, I wanted to continue. I felt I could always get better. I could always do more. Some days, I wanted to be on the national team. Some days, I was set on playing in Germany or Norway. I moved toward better leagues, more competitive teams. I moved from second division to first. Sometimes I just wanted to be on a top team, no matter where I had to live. Other days, I was satisfied to play in parks and alleys, I was happy to love playing, happy my body still worked well, happy I had my health. It was impossible to define success cleanly, impossible for success to mean the same thing to more than one person, or even for it to mean the same thing to me over time. But I always had the sense there was some threshold I hadn't crossed, some door I hadn't yet opened. Behind it was a room in which everything I desired took shape.

24'

WHEN I WAS VERY YOUNG, MY RELATIONSHIP TO SOCCER WAS simple. It existed without and before the language used to describe it. It was a flat and open plain with no sides. Soccer smelled like a clean T-shirt. Soccer clung to me the whole school day. At the drinking fountain, I breathed out heavily and soccer spread in the air, floating all around me. When I was seven years old and playing in the State Cup final, I scored a goal while putting my hair up into a ponytail. If my team was punished with fitness at practice, I smiled while running sprints, because I never got tired.

In third grade, my class wrote letters to our future selves. I never received mine in the mail, but I still remember what I wrote. At the time there was no professional league, so I could only say I wanted to play soccer in college. I also wrote that I wanted to be a writer and have two kids with boring names.

The same year, I tried to do all kinds of impossible things. I wrote letters to the president, marched against war, dug holes to the center of the Earth. For a long time, there was a photo of me pinned to the fridge in my childhood home; in it, duct tape is wrapped around my arms, cardboard wings affixed. I am poised to jump off of our trampoline and into the grass. I am trying to fly. I must have been old enough to know this stunt wouldn't work but young enough still to believe it might. To know the truth and not understand its limitations is the state of being a child. Like the striker's impulse to forget, youthful contemplation of the impossible cultivates a bullish and unlikely confidence. The longer I remained there, the longer I could play.

25'

WHEN I WAS GROWING UP, MY ROOM WAS COVERED IN POSTERS
of the University of Oregon football team. My favorite player
was the quarterback. On my door, I hung a full-page photo of
him I'd carefully clipped from *The Oregonian*. In the picture,
he has raised the ball and is leaning back slightly, poised and
confident before a throw. I scoured the team's roster on the day
of a game and discovered the smallest player was just five
foot ten. I thought to myself, *if I grow to be that tall, I can play
on the team*. My body, I thought at just nine years old, could still
grow beyond any limitation. My dad, eyeing the program in
my hand, didn't point out the shortest player's weight—one
hundred pounds heavier than mine would ever be.

In an article online titled "Physiological Differences Between Male and Female Athletes," I read: *male athletes have a
higher oxygen carrying capacity than women. . . . Male athletes have
longer and larger bones, Male athletes have a higher ratio of muscle
mass to body weight*.

I played football in the elementary schoolyard for years,

from the first light until the bell rang for classes to begin. The neighborhood boys and I tackled each other into shrubs while the sun rose. We dove for passes, spilling out of the grass onto the cement of the blacktop, skinning our knees and elbows. Eventually, when I explained to my parents that I wanted to play on a real team, my dad took me to a meeting at the middle school where I received the pads and helmet and registered for the fifth-grade team. I tried it all on immediately. I liked how much there was to arrange, how everything slid into place— knee pads, thigh pads, hip and tailbone protectors. There was a pocket for each bit of foam, each part of the armor. I liked the hooks and popping sounds the shoulder pads made when they locked in, I liked the chin strap that held the helmet firmly in place. On the car ride home from the meeting, my dad took off his T-shirt so I could put something over my new gear, and I liked how I felt, encased in plastic and foam, protected, solid. When we got home, he took a photo of me posing in the garden. I was ten. I would be the first girl to play for the team.

26'

FANS OF SOCCER OFTEN COMPLAIN ABOUT *FLOPPING* OR *DIVING*. When they want to draw a foul, players fall over after being lightly nudged or jostled. They roll and writhe after the slightest touch, grabbing their shin and contorting their faces into a silent scream. It's a dramatic performance meant to draw the attention of the referee. Flopping is a practiced strategy that frustrates many viewers. Brazil's Neymar Jr., one of the best players in the world, has a reputation for this behavior. I once read that he was taught the art of flailing as a young boy. His father wanted him to be able to protect himself. Neymar had always been one of the smallest players on the field.

I was never taught to draw a foul or fall to the ground after contact in the penalty box. Instead, I learned that it drew praise to keep going, to fight, and to endure through bodies and obstacles and tackles. Women never flop! It's not because we're philosophically opposed to the tactic, but because our toughness is our product and resilience helps prove the value of our efforts. There is no hiding that women athletes are, on the whole, slower and less capable of building muscle than our male counterparts. Our power manifests in subtler ways. In the world of sports, women must always remind ourselves, and anyone watching, that pain will not be the thing that impedes us.

I remember the first big hit I took at football practice, a helmet to my cold, bare leg that split my shin open. This, I thought, was part of the test. I stood up quickly and ignored the wound. By the end of practice, my sock was wet with a deep-red stain.

27'

I HAVE ALWAYS TAKEN A QUIET PRIDE IN MY BRUISES AND CUTS, which stretched and grew, changed color and shape as time passed. When I was playing soccer, I had scrapes on my knees, and, each day, new bumps collected on my shins. I ran my fingers over the permanent lumps of scar tissue that rested at the top of each of my ankles. I liked having physical proof that I had done something, I had tried hard, I had used my body. Out of season, my skin cleared, calluses softened, scratches and cuts retreated into pale scars that would eventually disappear. This seasonal healing always felt like a kind of loss.

During a game in Melbourne, I leapt up for a header, and an opponent's elbow collided with my cheekbone. The skin split without any resistance, and a fine, red slit underlined my eye. The referee stopped the game so we could clean up the blood, and I sat on the ground surrounded by teammates who were also nurses. A crowd of hands touched my cheek gently as they pulled the broken skin together with butterfly bandages. After the game, we drove to a doctor's office somewhere in the nearby suburbs, and our captain, Kristen, held the cut together with two fingers while a nurse sealed it with glue. When we walked outside, we saw the doctor smoking on a bench in the parking lot. He waved as we drove away. I sent my mom a selfie of my bandages, black eye, and pouting face. When I called her, she sounded upset on the phone. She asked about the hospital; she was worried about the care I'd received, and she also sounded concerned that the red line might mark my face forever. She must have been mourning the perfection of my skin, how it was when I was a young. When I went to a follow-up appointment at a bigger hospital downtown, the doctor lamented the glue, the fingers, the smoking attending. *If I'd been able to stitch this up*, she told me, *you wouldn't have ended up with a scar at all.*

28'

FOR AS LONG AS I CAN REMEMBER, I'VE ASSOCIATED PAIN WITH effort, equated physical expenditure with accomplishment. I still imagine that the sensation of bruising flesh is inseparable from the feeling of being fully alive.

I think of my mom: three childbirths with no epidural. I assume she wanted to be present for it, to live through it in all of its misery, to embrace this fact of womanhood. Maybe she thought it would prove something. My mother has never spoken much about her own pain, from childbirth or otherwise. For the most part, she is stoic and reserved. She was part of a generation of women who lived through a fledgling feminism and didn't grow up accustomed to its rewards. She played sports before Title IX protected female participants. She endured various injustices, and, in the end, she succeeded in remarkable ways: she was the first female partner at her law firm, a state champion 200-meter sprinter. I wonder if she felt her pain was a rite, as I had so many times throughout my athletic career.

In the space around my mother's suffering is a stillness, a

silence. Years after I quit soccer, I become pregnant, and I am determined to move through my labor without medication, for no other reason than to discover what is on the other side of great pain. I will think of pregnancy and childbirth as an athletic event. To endure is to *suffer patiently*. And I have been made to believe that the greatest reward awaits us after a struggle.

29'

IN THE UNITED STATES FOR A WEEK DURING A MIDSEASON break, I spent one afternoon watching the marathon from the roof of an apartment building in Seattle, where Cole had relocated for work. From where I sat, it looked like a parade. Colors, flags, the faint sound of cheering, and a seated crowd that looked like they had been waiting for something all morning. Fat runners, skinny runners, short, tall, old, young runners. There were runners with dogs, runners who walked, runners in groups and on their own. Some of them were running for a cause, for cancer, for their brother who passed away from a rare disease. Some ran to cross off a line item on their bucket list, or because they wanted to live longer, to stay healthy. All marathons vaguely commemorate the 25-mile run of Greek wartime messenger Pheidippides. After his journey, he burst into the assembly in Athens to announce *we have won*, collapsed, and died.

Women were effectively barred from running in the Boston Marathon until 1972, seventy-five years after the first race was run. The event was deemed too long, their bodies too fragile. The first-ever woman to run registered using just the initials of her first and middle names and competed with a numbered bib. In the middle of her race, an official grabbed at her shirt, trying to take her registration number during his assault. Her boyfriend, running alongside her, shoved him out of the way, onto the ground.

In 1977, a UCLA study published in *Nature* predicted women would outrun men in the marathon within five years. Since they had been permitted to race, women's performances improved at phenomenal rates. But the study's prediction was wrong. The gender gap closes farther out, at the edges of endurance sports, where the need for maximum muscular output is replaced with the demand that athletes persist through fatigue. In 100-plus-mile races, women can defeat men by ten hours or more. In 2013, a photo went viral of an endurance runner breastfeeding on the sidelines of a 110-mile race she went on to win.

Elite long-distance swimmers are also primarily women. In 2013, Diana Nyad swam from Florida to Cuba. It was her fifth attempt, and she was sixty-four years old. *Endurance is not a young person's game*, she said in an interview. *I thought I might even be better at sixty than I was at thirty. You have a body that's almost as strong, but you have a much better mind.* The athleticism demanded in ultra-long-distance events upends the usual logic of age and gender.

The effort required to endure can result in triumph and beauty. But it can also be devastating and traumatic. Endurance is not always rewarded. Lack of opportunity correlates with the need to persevere, to dissociate or comply. In the face of uncertainty, instability, and the perpetually ticking clocks of their professional careers, women soccer players have suffered low pay, abusive owners, and poor working conditions. I often recall watching replays of Kerri Strug finishing the vault in tears at the 1996 Summer Olympics. She landed on one leg after badly injuring her ankle and clinched the USA's gold medal in gymnastics.

30'

IT TOOK THE FOOTBALL COACHES A YEAR TO FIND AN EMPTY locker room for me in the middle school's basement. There, I dressed for games and practices alone in eerie silence. It was in one of these rooms, after a practice in the sixth grade, where I got my first period.

An athlete on her period is three times as likely to tear her ACL. An athlete on her period is more prone to exhaustion. An athlete on her period demands a higher caloric intake. An athlete on her period can easily become anemic. In my first year playing overseas, I stopped menstruating, and I felt thankful for one less variable. When a fellow professional told me she hadn't gotten her period since she was fourteen, I sensed a hidden pride. She had outrun her fertility; she had triumphed over her body. There is a name for this phenomenon: hypothalamic amenorrhea. Training at an elite level increases testosterone and eliminates estrogen. The condition can cause wide-ranging complications: osteoporosis, heart disease, and infertility among them.

Sports scientists have only recently begun to investigate how players should manage their training during disruptive periods of their menstrual cycle. Usually, teams prefer to speak quickly and quietly about the subject. In a meeting with her national team, my teammate was handed a bag full of birth control pills and instructed to take one every day. They were enough to last her the year.

Discipline shaped our bodies in other ways, too. We measured our percentage of body fat and oxygen intake. We measured our heart rate. How low is your pulse when you wake up? How high is it during training? How much oxygen is in your blood, and how much of it do you utilize when you're at a full sprint? Over time, I developed an arrhythmia that my doctor back home told me was normal for elite athletes. My heart beat rapidly at random moments throughout the day. Sometimes, the humming vibration in my chest made me cough. I imagined it was worse when I drank coffee and for two weeks, I committed to ordering green tea from the café before games instead of an Americano.

In the middle school basement, I stepped out of my football uniform to shower. I felt a sticky warmth between my legs and saw the bloodstain. I can still remember the exact pair of white American Apparel boy briefs I was wearing. But most of all, I remember this sudden knowledge: I wouldn't be able to play football much longer. Soon, the boys were going to be faster than me, stronger, taller. I would end up quitting football after my first year of high school to avoid injury and to prioritize soccer. But this moment, years earlier, was the beginning of a fundamental inequality between our bodies. In front of a full-length mirror in the locker room, I studied my own reflection; I stood on one side of a threshold looking back at the gift of my girlhood, of shameless, uninhibited play.

31'

FOR SOME REASON, IT BECAME HARDER TO SPEAK MY DREAMS aloud as I got older. *I want to play professional soccer. I want to play professional soccer.* I hesitated when filling out customs or hospital forms, I paused any time I had to fill in a box asking me to state my occupation. The experience of playing overseas was cloistered and invisible, opportunities in the US were coveted and few. Professional Women's Soccer Player sounded impossible and grandiose. Maybe the unease was fear, a change of heart, self-consciousness, or something else. But it's probably simpler than that: as soon as you speak your desires out loud, you become responsible to them.

I always envied players who didn't seem to have this problem. Some women I knew were unfettered in their ambition, unembarrassed by its scope, unintimidated by the commitment it demanded. There is a difference between what is impossible and what is extremely unlikely. I think of twenty-four-year-old Paige, an opponent of mine in Korea and a friend there. When she was just six, she was determined to go to the University of

North Carolina. She grew up watching Mia Hamm, a Tar Heel, play in the 1999 World Cup. When Paige graduated from high school, she walked onto the soccer team at UNC without a scholarship and became captain by her senior year. When she graduated, she was drafted into the NWSL. On a walk one afternoon, I asked her what she wanted. She responded without hesitating: she wanted to be a starting player on an American club team. She wanted to play on the US national team. Her goals were ambitious, concrete, committed, and unafraid.

I wished I could say there was only one thing in this life I wanted to be.

32'

ON A PARTICULAR NIGHT OF PRACTICE IN HIGH SCHOOL, IT was damp and late enough to be dark. A blinding circle of artificial light illuminated the field. We couldn't see anything but the green rectangle of carpet-like grass. My soccer team practiced at the University of Portland, the collegiate home of my childhood heroes. I was smiling and laughing and bubbling with confidence, the way I always felt when I played.

How many sports are you playing right now? the coach pulled me aside to ask.

I played football, lacrosse, and softball, and I ran track. I knew what was coming: the demand to consolidate, to constrain myself.

If you committed yourself to soccer, you could be one of the greatest. He paused. *I'm telling you this so that, ten years down the road, you don't wish someone had.*

The word *greatest* rolled in my head. I must have responded with not much more than a nod. I felt paralyzed by an unfamiliar combination of pride, confusion, regret, responsibility, and the distinctly childish feeling of not wanting to disappoint an adult who believed in me.

I think the word he was toying with, the one he was implying but not saying aloud, was *potential*. The opposite of potential is *actual*. As in *real, existing*. Potential is fantasy, all of its possibilities dependent on how long we can nurture the unknown. The future orientation of the word both excited and paralyzed me. Beyond the fantasy was the persistent and haunting suggestion that the strengths and shortcomings of my own body were hidden from me. I still can't think of a notion more privately threatening. Before we set out, it's impossible to know what we're capable of. Then it is just as difficult to recognize when we have reached the limits of our ability.

33'

NOTHING CLOSES SO SWIFTLY OR SURELY AS THE WINDOW OF time in which you are in the prime for your sport. Track and field: twenty-five. Swimming: twenty-two. Marathon: thirty. Gymnastics: sixteen. Soccer: twenty-six. Most sports have a scientifically proven peak age, although my older teammates always insisted that thirty-two was the new twenty-seven.

34'

23: I spent my twenty-third birthday moving out of my host family's house and into a shotgun rental in the warehouse district of Melbourne. My beautiful and generous host mother dropped off a cake with my last suitcase, and I shared it with my new roommates, strangers to me, at our kitchen table as the refrigerator hummed and rain fell against a sliding glass door.

24: It snowed that April in Sweden. My teammates decorated my locker with my favorite candies: rich Swedish chocolate and gummies from the bulk section of the grocery store. After practice, a group of us walked to the lake, still partially frozen over, and skipped rocks against its surface until our hands and feet got too cold. Back in my apartment, I watched a video of a Swedish physicist skating on black ice. His gliding made high-pitched, tinny sounds on the frozen water. The people there call this *wild ice skating*. Hobbyist skaters glide down rivers and lakes when they are covered in a precariously thin layer of ice. The skaters are often mathematicians and scientists who have calculated their risk and measured the trips carefully. The ice can be as thin as two inches. It's actually the water below that supports the weight of a skater and prevents the ice from cracking.

25: I ate a slice of white cake on the floor of a restaurant with the team in Korea. We crossed our legs under the table and ate the dessert with chopsticks, licking frosting from their metal tips. That evening, I got the flu, or some short-lived fever, and could barely make it to my bed from the bus. The birthday was made worse when I learned people in Korea count years of life differently. When I said *I am twenty-five today*, I was corrected by my teammates. *It's twenty-six in Korean years*. There, the day you are born you are already one.

35'

THE HAZE THAT SURROUNDED OUR COMPOUND IN KOREA WAS stifling and heavy. Morning fog was hard to distinguish from smog, a close partner in appearance and name. Everyone here claimed that the pollution blew across the ocean from Beijing; it was China's fault. But I could see some of it wafting up into the sky across the bay from the factories in Seoul. It came from every direction. When the sky was blue, it was blue only above my head in a vertical strip. The horizon was always cushioned by a yellow-gray blur. My roommate closed the windows to avoid pollutants and pulled the curtains so she could nap. When she traveled home and I was alone on our off-weekends, I opened the balcony doors and let the room fill with air and light.

There are methods to combat the unfair and unrelenting force of time. My teammates in Korea used toner and exfoliant. They wore sunscreen in the winter, long-sleeve shirts and gloves in the summer heat. When we traveled, each of them packed a bag full of lotions and creams and unloaded them onto the hotel bureau, a lineup of beauty and ritual.

As athletes age, reaction times diminish, hearts fail, lungs struggle, muscles weaken, and ligaments lose their elasticity. Injuries accumulate. But Serena Williams played in a Grand Slam final at thirty-seven, Tom Brady was forty-three when he won his seventh Super Bowl, Carli Lloyd played in the Olympics at the age of thirty-nine. Brady would probably attribute his success at an older age to holistic training and a rigid diet (the TB12 method). I've read that LeBron James spends more than a million dollars a year on his at-home rehab facilities. This budget includes the employment of a personal biomechanist and the use of various experimental treatments for inflammation and pain. Older players can also change their style of play. If you compare them to their younger selves, they run, jump, and move less; they become opportunists. Eventually, of course, all of these efforts fall short.

The day after my twenty-fifth birthday, in Korea, two of my teammates took me to the mall and presented me with a range of lotions and tinctures. They had names like Skin Milk and Moon Glow. They sounded lush and comforting. The creams had mysterious and intriguing ingredients: turtle shell, snail, horse hair, ash. My teammates instructed me to first put on toner, then to apply the lotion in gentle circles. They told me to use my weakest two fingers, so as to protect the delicate and aging skin around my eyes.

36'

AMERICANS OFTEN SAY THEY FIND SOCCER BORING, TOO SLOW. Maybe that's why it has failed to take hold in the United States the same way it has in other countries. So much work for so little reward! Often there are no goals, and many minutes can go by without even a single scoring opportunity. The best player in the world, Lionel Messi, is sometimes criticized by spectators for walking too much during his games. To them, it must seem like laziness or apathy. Messi runs, on average, more than a mile less than his teammates in every game.

In a soccer life, time is marked in unique ways—there are no Mondays or Fridays; instead we have game days, recovery days, training days, rest days. There are seasons, but only two of them: off-season and in-season. Days of the week are irrelevant. Moods, too, oscillate uniquely. After a win, I was buoyed for days. On the other hand, with nothing else to distract me, no family or friends to summon, a loss consumed me completely. I watched footage from games, replayed missed shots and mistakes. The only thing that promised to uplift me was another game.

Off the field, there was a lot of waiting. We waited for training, waited for game day, waited for planes, waited for the season to start, and waited to go home again after it ended. Years flew by, but days inched forward. In Lithuania, I wrote to pass time in the empty mornings. I sat at the kitchen table until my housemates arose—Noel at nine to eat yogurt and cereal, Megan well after that to make an omelet at ten thirty. We filled our days with familiar patterns in an unfamiliar city; eating kaneles at the corner café, walking in circles around the supermarket, riding our bikes to the team's gym. Some of us took online classes; some sunbathed and played video games. Some watched TV and scrolled on their phones until practice. Some developed gambling habits, drank too much. Leisure was something to manage. This much rest for the body was essential; for the mind, it could be unbearable. On the worst days, the first thing I did when I woke up was mark an X through the day on the calendar.

37'

TO FILL THE IDLE TIME, I GOOGLED SOME OF THE GIRLS I'D
grown up playing with and tried to figure out where they ended
up. I wondered how their time on the field translated to their
new lives, if they had learned to utilize their old skills, or if
their soccer selves were just gone. A few of these women had
been much better players than me. They went to Division I
colleges, sprinted faster than I did, had more confidence, scored
more goals in high school. But they weren't playing anymore.
The "mother" of my high school team, who always had extra
prewrap and a kind word, was the assistant director at a summer camp in our hometown. The striker who towered over everyone and always found herself in the right place to score goals
was now an analyst at a big retail company. The fiercest defender I knew—loud, powerful, and unforgiving on the field—
was pregnant and getting married. She had bought a house in
the suburbs of Philadelphia. It looked like another woman had
taken a coaching job. She claimed it was just a hiatus, but I was
doubtful she would play again.

I obsessed over exit interviews and retirement announcements I found on players' social media accounts or club websites. Some people needed to make more money, some got injured, some were so old they just slowed down, some were sick of living out of a suitcase, some found another calling. Reading the announcements was like scouring an obituary for the cause of death, not always mentioned. I saw my own inevitable future hidden in their decisions, and I was waiting for whichever end was to be mine. The mix of what I felt while reading: empathetic, disappointed, superior. They had not lasted.

38'

WHEN I LANDED IN STOCKHOLM AT THE START OF A NINE-
month season, the team's manager met me and my new roommate at the airport. He grabbed our bags, and we drove together,
exhausted, across the lake-filled flatness of Götaland. *We love
Americans, because they really want to win*, he said during the
car ride.

My nationality always preceded me. American players were
supposed to be tall and strong. An American in Korea once told
me that her team's coaching staff hadn't been able to hide their
disappointment when they first saw her get off the plane standing only five foot five. Americans should be aggressive players;
they should be physically dominant and emotionally resilient.
Above all, Americans should be tenaciously and unrelentingly
competitive.

The manager kept an eye on us in the rearview mirror, smiling. I tried not to nod off; I wanted to give the impression of
strength and resolve, but the jet lag was overwhelming, and my
head bounced against the glass of the window as I dozed.

When we pulled into the town square, he asked if we would pose so he could take a photo for the team's website. They wanted to announce our arrival. Lake Möckeln pushed small waves against a cold sand beach. The water was just a few minutes' walk from our apartment. Late in the season, when the lake froze around the edges, we would hang our legs off the dock to soothe them in the frigid water—a makeshift ice bath. On that first day in February, it was unseasonably warm, and a little bit of sun peeked through the overcast sky. We held our freshly printed jerseys up to our chests and stood with the water behind us, smiling.

The Damallsvenskan, Sweden's top league, was the first women's domestic professional league in the world. It has existed in some form since 1988. But my team played in the semi-professional Division 2. Almost all of my teammates had to work before or after practice. During the day, they were teachers, bakers, policewomen, and caregivers. After practice, they were babysitters, bartenders, grocery store clerks. It was the luxury of the international players, the only ones on fully professional contracts, to sit and wait for training, to kill time. I occupied myself by biking to the local library, sitting in the lone café in the town square, or swimming in the lake. My roommate rewatched all of *Friends* and called home daily.

When we trained in the evenings, I could tell the other women were more tired than I was. They arrived at the field after a full day of working, caring for a family, living an adult life. One day, I yelled at a teammate for misplacing an easy pass.

It has got to be better! My own voice startled me: angry, confident, demanding—distinctly American. She stopped, looked at me, and was poised to yell back, but, at the last minute, she just rolled her eyes and walked away. She must have thought that I couldn't possibly understand.

39'

BUT I KNEW HER EXHAUSTION, IN A WAY. DURING MY FIRST season in Australia, in addition to playing, I worked a job in order to be paid anything by the club. A visa stipulation, or something. Most Saturdays, I ran to catch the train two blocks from my house to coach a seven a.m. game in the suburbs of Melbourne. It was July, the dead of winter in the Southern Hemisphere, so I left the house wrapped in a puffy parka and kept my hands in my pockets. I made thirty dollars per hour coaching and helping the club with marketing. I stalked the sidelines, cajoled parents, cheered and instructed nine-year-old boys and twelve-year-old girls at weekly practices and games. On the mornings when I coached, I ate eggs and avocado from a Tupperware container so I wasn't too hungry by ten a.m., when I walked to a nearby field to play with my team in the second-division Women's Premier League.

In this league, we made nothing for playing, while our male counterparts in the same division took home more than $1,000 a week. A shocking disparity, but not unusual. Even in the seventh division, the men were paid *something* for each game. At the club's office, where I sometimes worked extra hours, I commiserated loudly with my teammate about this pay gap. The director overheard and asked us, with an impossibly stiff smile, why it was we measured our self-worth in money. We should be thankful. We were lucky to be here. I wondered how long he would stay at his job if he were compensated only with warm feelings.

On other days, my job for the club was to write newsletters or coach clinics at local schools. I was exhausted by groups of children and didn't yet think of myself as a mentor or a coach. As we yelled and encouraged, jumped and ran around gyms across the city, I wondered if I was saving up enough energy for training later that day.

40'

Australia: AUD 30 (US$30) per hour, 30 hours/week, for "coaching," flights, homestay

Sweden: SEK 5,000 (US$500) per month, housing, flights, lunch and dinner every day

Korea: WON 50,000,000 (US$37,000) per year, housing, all meals, flights

Lithuania: EUR 1,100 EUR (US$1,200) per month, housing, flights, one meal per day, car

Norway: NOK 18,000 (US$1,685) per month, housing, flights

41'

EVEN WHILE I ENJOYED SOCCER, THE INTERNAL MONOLOGUE was persistent: *I should get a real job. I should settle down somewhere. I should move closer to my family. I should spare my body. I shouldn't take soccer so seriously. I should acknowledge I have wasted time. There is no money in women's sports, there is no future.*

I kept two résumés on my desktop. One was for my playing career, and one was for real work—that is, what I did when I was not playing or what I might do some day. That one was for job applications I submitted in moments of uncertainty and pause. Teaching, nonprofits, museums, marketing firms, law school? Dreams were meant to be chased only until you wake up. Sport could seem frivolous. *Real life needs to begin sometime,* I can remember my dad saying when I talked about quitting. He meant it as a comfort. *You had a good run.*

Once, between seasons, my cousin offered to get me an interview at the company where he worked. When I followed up, he sent me a message asking me for a revision: *Can you move the soccer thing to the very top of your résumé? They really like hiring athletes.* I wondered what they thought they were sure to get if they hired me. Competitive, hardworking, willing to sacrifice almost anything for abstract rewards. I wanted to respond and tell him that I was not like most athletes. But I wasn't sure this was true. Instead, I took his advice, padded my resume with more soccer accolades, was offered the job, and turned it down right away.

But I did have to find odd jobs to make ends meet. When I returned to Minneapolis from Karlskoga, I worked four blocks from my house at the American Swedish Institute. My qualifications included the fact that I had recently lived in Sweden. Before Christmas, I was tasked with putting price stickers on all of the holiday merchandise. The store sold Dala horses and patterned sponges, dripless candles and coasters made from bisected birch trunks. I stood hunched over a wide table, timing myself peeling, placing, sticking, peeling, placing, sticking, for eight hours each day. I worked up a sweat in the basement room. The stooped position caused pain in my legs and back, and the other employees offered me a chair, but I knew I would be slower if I sat, so I declined.

I spent a different offseason working for a nonprofit, vaguely applying the skills I'd acquired with my undergraduate English degree by writing newsletters and editing marketing copy. I printed thousands of pamphlets and folded them along perfect lines. At the end of each day, I was exhausted.

I'd sit down on the couch and eat like an animal, watching reruns of *Top Chef* before falling into a deep sleep. In one episode, the contestants were moved to tears while talking about their late mentor, who had continued to work in the kitchen even as his body was progressively debilitated by ALS. They spoke of how he showed up in the restaurant for premeal tastings even when he could no longer lift his own fork. He worked until he died. To me, their tears looked like ones of admiration, inspiration, aspiration. They would like to think they'd do the same.

Of all the jobs I had, I preferred those that involved manual labor. I spent several offseasons working on farms and vineyards, where progress was measured neatly, by row. There were eighty rows in a bloc, and fifteen blocs on the property where I spent a few months pruning vines and pulling up rogue blackberry shoots. I calculated that it would take me five hours and twelve minutes to trim all of the vines in a single bloc. I moved steadily, obsessively, with my head down. I didn't notice when the sun dipped below the pond, or when a rain cloud dusted the hill across the valley. I beamed when my boss asked how I could have possibly trimmed all of the vines so quickly.

My name, Georgia, is of Greek origin. The name originally meant "farmer." It comes from *ge*, meaning "earth," and *ergon*, meaning "work." Even though I farmed irregularly, I have always identified with the origin of my name. I have absorbed its significance, just as I always secretly believed my sisters' names, meaning "grace" and "dark one," seemed to predict something about their lives. To work the earth, to use your body to create something, to labor manually, to be grounded in the seasons and mired in repetition. This all felt true to my experience of the world.

42'

BETWEEN SEASONS, TRAINING WAS DONE ALONE IN STOLEN slivers of time before and after my various part-time jobs. To be consistent required a certain work ethic and discipline, of which I was very proud. Unlike contract negotiations, agent deals, injuries, or starting spots, I could control how much I practiced and how much I prepared. So, I fixated on fitness and my first touch. There is an encyclopedia in my mind of every public track, every lengthy staircase, every park with a concrete wall in every town where I've lived. Early in the morning, before even the city attendants were at work: one hundred touches each on the left foot, the right foot, the top of the foot, the bottom of the foot, the outside. Then start over again. I loved spending time with the ball in this way. In the end, I would have touched its surface a thousand times and thought to myself, *if nothing else, at least I've done this today.* Training for soccer every day felt tangibly productive. I was grounded by the repetition.

43'

AT SIXTEEN, I'D JUST ACQUIRED MY DRIVER'S LICENSE, AND with it came the duty of driving myself to and from soccer practice in the suburbs. The forty-five-minute journey was emblematic of teen freedom. I sped, I talked on the phone, I sang along to my music, listening as loud as I wanted. One particular night after training, I climbed into my dad's station wagon to go home and put on "Hoppípolla," by Sigur Rós, the kind of melodramatic song that might play in a movie as a car drives off a cliff. In the next two months, I would have to decide whether to go to college primarily to play soccer or to prioritize academics. On the brink of adulthood, I felt for the first time that I had at least two selves, and I anticipated that they might be incompatible. On this particular evening, a conversation with my coach made the emotions of the decision surface. He'd vaguely encouraged me to walk on to the local college team, which he coached. It was one of the top programs in the country, a team I had admired since I was a young girl. I'd already been accepted to a school I loved with a lower-division team that was much less competitive. My coach's encouragement was paralyzing. When the driver in front of me slowed to a stop, I was crying and no longer paying attention. I slammed on my brakes, but the two teammates behind me didn't have as much time to react. No one was hurt, so the jolt from the crash felt like a gift: it offered me a tangible, physical excuse for my tears, for my shaking and confusion. It calmed me down.

In the following days, I asked my two favorite high school English teachers what I should do. One of them told me not to waste time, to *get to work on your mind*. This one liked to call me a jock. I looked up the exact meaning: *an enthusiastic athlete or sports fan, especially one with few other interests*. The word might have once been short for jockey or jock strap. It might have originally been a nickname for Jack or a word meant to indicate a *common man*. There was once a feminized version, *jockette*. I spent the majority of my free time, and my most joyful hours, playing sports. But still, *jock* felt like a catchall for a vast group of people. The word didn't begin to attend to all of our disparate motivations, joys, pains, and desires.

The other teacher told me to pursue soccer now because *you have the rest of your life to read*.

This contradiction was the heart of my experience.

44'

IT WAS JANUARY WHEN I ARRIVED IN SOUTH KOREA FOR MY third professional season, and snow plows still needed to clear our training fields. The subzero wind bit my naked hands, and, on the second morning of practice, a teammate gave me a pair of her gloves. A sullen heaviness accompanied our training, which took place every day of the week, twice. *Apa* (sick), *chua* (cold), *baegopa* (hungry) were some of the first Korean words I learned. I was on my first contract in a top league, and I was making a living wage. Alone in my hotel room during preseason, I wondered if I was good enough to be there, I wondered if I was worth the money, and I wondered if I could last the year. *Himduro*, they taught me: difficult.

For most of the season, the team was housed in one wing of a compound on an artificial island in the Yellow Sea. Inside, each bedroom door closed with an electronic padlock, and the hallway smelled of perfumed laundry detergent. At high tide, waves reached the edge of our building, which was secured by a tall gate that locked every night at ten.

The rest of the building was made up of halls of empty classrooms, conference rooms, and offices. In the languid evenings, I wandered vacant corridors and opened each door I passed. In one of the rooms, there was a long table covered in a fake-wood veneer and surrounded by plump, leather office chairs. An artificial fig tree sat in the corner, where it got no light, and an always-blank TV screen was mounted to one wall. The others were bare. I pushed a desk against the window, unburdened my backpack of its books, pens, and paper, and sat where I could see the dramatic tide recede, leaving dinghies and cargo ships stuck in vast mudflats. I watched as the boat owners disembarked and scoured the ocean bottom for clams.

I opened my notebook and drew the diagram of a simple sentence. *The waves broke on the shore.* I used lines and dashes to depict the grammar structure. A visual representation of the way words relate to each other is a lot like the picture of bodies arranged on a soccer field. On the page across from the sentence, I sketched the corner kick we had learned at practice that day: a small rectangle for the six-yard box, a larger one for the eighteen, and a pair of tick marks for the goalmouth. A team of Xs moved across the page into open space, a dotted line for a run, a solid line for a pass. They were verbs, adjectives, subjects, falling away from each other.

I tried to write, but I could feel my left calf twinging with the threat of injury, my head throbbed, my blistered heels pressed into the sharp edge of my tennis shoes. I hadn't drunk enough water that day. We had practice early the next morning and then a flight to Tokyo, where we were scheduled to play three games in five days. When I was first starting out, I thought a professional soccer career might give me time to write. I thought playing would provide the balance and flexibility that a full-time job didn't. But in reality, it was impossible to spend so much time prioritizing my body and, at the same time, to reside in the private world of my mind. I followed the team to dinner, to practice, to the shower, to the bus. Words were quieted by my body, which demanded incredible amounts of focus and attention.

When I was living in Sweden, I tried to write in the mornings at the public library. I sat by a window overlooking the town square—two restaurants, a bank, a night club. In Lithuania, I took notes in my room, spreading paper and books out on the king size bed. In Norway, I pulled a desk up to my window, which overlooked a fjord. In Australia, I read a lot and wrote nothing.

When I sift through diaries I kept while I was playing, I find a page dated *July 7, 2016, Incheon.* The only text on the page: *I am too tired to write, there is nothing in my brain.*

45'

IN EMPTY ROOMS, LIBRARIES, AND CAFÉS, I PAGED THROUGH my worn copy of *The Waves*. I thought of how I related to Woolf's Percival. I felt an ambiguous affinity with him when I read. I was defensive of his character. I tried to emulate his focus, his singularity. Neville narrates: *He will throw off his coat and stand with his legs apart, with his hands ready, watching the wicket. And he will pray, "Lord let us win"; he will think of one thing only.* The only thing to consider was how to score a goal; the only thing to do was to win.

The characterization of Percival reminded me of an essay by David Foster Wallace in which he reviewed the poorly written autobiography of tennis player Tracy Austin. Wallace explains: *those who receive and act out the gift of athletic genius must, perforce, be blind and dumb about it.* By *dumb*, he is referring, in part, to the complete presence of mind that allows an elite athlete to silence any narrative impulse and perform even in the most difficult of circumstances. In an interview I once watched on YouTube, American soccer player Sarah Woldmoe responded to a question about the skills required for her midfield position by saying: *if you've gotten the ball, and you're trying to think, you're too late.* Her statement backs up Wallace's theory that would have us believe there is *a difference in communicability,* even to the self, *between thinking and doing, between doing and being.* Dumbness, Wallace explains, the inarticulate nature of athletic geniuses, is not the *price* of their gift but its *essence.* In other words, a *genius-in-motion* can't also be a *genius-in-reflection.*

If we agree with Wallace, it follows that an athletic genius will not be able to write a good book. The wonder of their physical ability is, in part, reliant on wordlessness. It's the same with Percival, who doesn't speak, not even once, in *The Waves.* What goes through the elite athlete's mind at an important moment in their performance, Wallace guesses, *might be nothing at all.*

I cringe when I listen to vacuous postgame interviews with athletes. At the end of a football game, I turn off the TV before the star speaks to the camera; I am quick to avoid confirmation of Wallace's stance. I want to believe that the internal life of an athlete can be complicated and verbose. I know my position is tenuous, often contradicted by the behavior of people whose lives revolve around sports. But I also believe that asking an athlete to speak on their performance after its conclusion is like asking a sculptor to play the piano about an exhibition. These are faulty grounds on which to judge either one.

I've heard writers describe the sense that they don't know what they are writing until they are done, until the poem is in front of them, until the novel has concluded. They report being overtaken by a creative force, hearing voices. It is a supernatural experience, at odds with introspection and self-consciousness. *Poetry comes as a gift from powers beyond my will*, writes May Sarton in *Journal of a Solitude*. I am envious. I long for that but don't find it here. As I write this, I take up Neville's position at the top of a grassy hill, where he marvels at his friend. I study Percival, love him, romanticize his stoicism. I try to write with physical discipline at my desk, sitting upright, working my way toward completion.

HALFTIME

WHEN FORTY-FIVE MINUTES HAVE PASSED, THE MOOD IN THE locker room is more repair than preparation. We are getting ready *again* rather than *before*. If the day is humid or hot, we might change our uniforms completely. We will put on a fresh shirt and clean shorts for the beginning of the second half. We might check that the tape has held on our ankles, that our blisters are still covered with bandages. If we need to refuel, we should drink electrolytes and eat bananas or gummy worms. We will rest in hard plastic chairs, teasing our legs with too short of a break. We pull back our hair again into sweat-slicked ponytails and tighten the laces on our cleats. There might be large-scale revisions if the game's plan has not gone as intended. The coach will speak to the group and then to individual players. We will try to agree on what we need to do better.

When forty-five minutes have passed, we will do our best to become reinvigorated, we will walk back out onto the field with a renewed, if damaged, hope.

46'

A SOCCER BALL IS OFTEN ANTHROPOMORPHIZED. IT *GOES BEG-GING, crawls, tempts*. The ball *teases* across the face of the goal. The ball *burns worms*, the ball *soars*, the ball is a *friend* or an *enemy*. The ball is *delicious*, the ball *has a mind of its own*. I remember playing with a soccer ball in the yard of my childhood home. If you kicked too hard, it would roll down a bank of shrubs and onto the street. From there, it sped down more hills and around a corner. I'd go sprinting after it as soon as I noticed, trying not to lose sight of it.

In *Soccer in Sun and Shadow*, Eduardo Galeano writes that most Latin American players refer to the soccer ball as a woman. *This ball here helped me a lot*, one player says. *She or her sisters, right? It is a family to whom I owe a debt of gratitude. Because without her nobody plays at all.*

A coach from my youth once told me that she hoped I'd eventually find a way to give back to the game, to repay this debt. I was never sure what she meant. Had I stolen something from soccer? Had I been selfish? For a long time, I believed that my coach had it backward. We gave soccer our time, and perhaps it was the sport which owed us for our hours of training and traveling, for abstinence and discipline and sacrifice. Soccer owed us something; we, who had measured our entire self-worth in fleeting moments of elation, needed to be repaid.

But in some moments, I really was overwhelmed by unmitigated gratitude. Ambition, negotiation, tough-minded feminism, these gave way to moments of childish joy. What, other than soccer, had I loved so unconditionally, for so long?

Sometimes I thought to myself, this must be the easiest job in the world. It was so easy to run around, to get paid to kick a ball, to do something I loved. It was easy to travel for free, to wear a uniform every day (red top with blue bottoms on Mondays, Wednesdays, and Fridays, navy top with black shorts on Tuesdays and Thursdays), to take extra naps. It was easy to tell people *I am chasing my dreams*, because they would always be impressed and encouraging. It was easy to imagine doing this for one more year, just one more year, and then another. It was easy being healthy and strong. It was easy to set my feet on the floor in the morning and, after a quick stretch, take another step.

47'

IN HIS SEMINAL BOOK, *THE GIFT*, LEWIS HYDE WRITES THAT any gift, including that of creativity, must remain in motion. A gift needs to be given away in order not to wither, suffer, disappear; you shouldn't cling to it too closely. And an artist must labor in gratitude in order to invoke their gift. Their labor might take the form of time, study, practice. In turn, when the proper moment arises, they are prepared and capable of giving the gift of their artistry to the world.

Similarly, a gifted athlete might be fast, strong, skilled. They are given toward physical abilities that they invoke through rigorous training—they can catch, throw, breathe, run, kick, fight in extraordinary ways. *You could be one of the greatest.* But athletes, like artists, have to labor for their craft. They have to sacrifice and practice discipline in order to come into their gift, to be able to share it with those who care to watch.

One Sunday in Seoul, Paige took me to a church where the parishioners spoke English. I don't believe in God, but I liked Paige, and I could understand her loneliness, so I went. The church was on the third floor of a high-rise and, for the service, about a hundred people were gathered in a windowless room. There was singing. We all shook hands and listened to music. As I observed, I thought of the conversations Paige and I had when we stayed up late at night in her apartment talking about the meaning of life and of soccer. I once asked her why she was still playing. She told me she played for His glory. She felt that she was in possession of *God's gift*, and she owed it to Him to keep playing.

On my way home after the church service, I walked alone through Gangnam streets lined with skyscrapers and wondered who I was serving.

48'

ON VACATION AFTER MY CONTRACT EXPIRED IN LITHUANIA, I visited Spain with Cole. We bought tickets to an FC Barcelona game just so we could say we'd seen Lionel Messi play in person. We found the cheapest tickets we could and sat at the very top of the full stadium where we could see the field and also, over the top of the stands, the city; its low-slung buildings sprawled all the way to the sea. It was a rare loss for the Spanish team. Barcelona fell 3–4.

In general, I am slow to cry and quick to goosebumps. But a beautiful moment in sports can send a shiver down my spine or cause a tear to well up in my eye. After an artist performs, the world looks different. A real artist brings something new, something completely unique to the world. The fans in Barcelona knew this about Messi. They understood all that he had given in his long career. Messi didn't do anything special in the game we watched, but that wasn't the point. He would find a way some other day. The 80,000 people in the stands, the kids with his name on the back of their jerseys were there to say *thank you, thank you, thank you.*

49'

DURING PRESEASON IN SEATTLE, OUR COACH SHOWED US AN
inspirational video and introduced his coaching philosophy. *In
our club,* he said, *we divide the players into warriors and artists.
We know the artist will change the game with one idea. We are willing to do whatever it takes to help the artist be at her best.* In other
words: the artist has a gift; the rest need to work hard.

It's hard to explain what the difference is. But there is a difference. Ashley dribbled like sand falling through a closed fist.
Time and motion followed different rules. The ball obeyed her,
it did whatever she commanded, even the impossible things. She
was on the Australian national team when she was fifteen, and
then tore her ACL three times. After she injured the knee once
more, playing with my team in Australia, she never touched
the ball again. Megan was famous by the time I met her. At
training, she laughed and joked. Her art was an animated pleasure and a joy, a playfulness. When she struck the ball, it played
along, bending through the air in incalculable arcs.

On the other hand, the warrior might go unnoticed by a

casual spectator. Lucy played the beautiful game in an ugly way. She used her body as a weapon, as a shield, as an object. Matea ran and ran and ran, wherever she could and whenever she needed to. The warrior will keep tackling, keep heading the ball, keep fighting, even with little reward, because they know their efforts are in service of something, or someone, larger than themselves.

50'

SOCCER IS KNOWN AROUND THE WORLD AS *THE BEAUTIFUL game*. There is no clear origin for this concept, though many associate the phrase with Brazilian soccer and Pelé, in particular. There are two Portuguese phrases that get conflated—*jogo bonito* (beautiful game) and *joga bonito* (play beautifully). I like the way these two ideas complement and contradict each other. *We are willing to do whatever it takes to help the artist be at her best.* There is a difference between the collective artistry of a team and the gift of an individual. Is it the game which is itself beautiful and artistic? Or are the players on the field responsible for the aesthetic product?

In *Games: Agency as Art*, C. Thi Nguyen argues that the design of a game itself—its rules, boundaries and goals—is what constitutes art. If a painter's medium is paint, a writer's medium language, a game's medium is agency. A game allows its players the freedom, grace, and opportunity to experience the power of their abilities.

51'

TRYING TO ASSEMBLE A SOCCER TEAM FOR THE SUMMER, I asked a friend if she would join. We needed girls, we always needed more girls. *I'm an artist*, she replied with a wry smile. I took a moment to think through her response. She must have meant that she doesn't play sports, or isn't athletic, or doesn't consider herself to be someone who is capable of contributing to the team, or she is simply uninterested. I wanted to tell her, *me too!* But instead, I just laughed. In his essay, David Foster Wallace admits to hiding Tracy Austin's memoir under a stack of more highbrow books as he checked out at the bookstore. It is very common to think of an interest in sports as antithetical to an interest in artistic pursuits.

In graduate school I wrote about anything but soccer and escaped my cohort every evening to play with the college's men's club team. I've always inhabited these two worlds, and I have also always lacked the language, confidence, or understanding to know how they inform each other and overlap. Maybe that is what I'm trying to reveal by writing this.

52'

SOCCER PLAYERS LOVE TO REPEAT THE MAXIM *LOVE WHAT YOU do, and you will never work a day in your life.* I read it in social media captions, blogs, and interviews. I've seen the quote attributed to Mark Twain, Confucius, and Tim Cook. It seems like a string of words that has no origin, and it describes a fundamental part of capitalism and American ideals. The nebulous form of passion is compacted and packaged to fit the shape of a job.

Then what is the price of mixing up a dream with work? Things must change when you start getting paid for something you used to do for fun, for free. In her collection of essays *Having and Being Had*, Eula Biss writes: *if art became my job, I'm afraid that would disturb my universe. I would have nothing unaccountable left in my life, nothing worthless.* Galeano writes something similar about the creative nature of soccer: *When the sport became an industry, the beauty that blossoms from the joy of play got torn out by its very roots.* He continues, *professional soccer con-*

demns all that is useless, and useless means not profitable. The result, he claims, is *a soccer of lightning speed and brute strength, a soccer that negates joy, kills fantasy and outlaws daring.*

In the typical professional contract, the unit of pay is one month, and the contract length is a single season. A player is paid for their time. Athletes in Korea give up most of their formal education at the age of twelve. Starting then, sport is their main focus. They often train three times a day in college, where they major in soccer. Upon graduation, soccer players hope to secure a spot on one of the eight teams that make up the WK League, the professional league where women soccer players can make a more stable wage than is offered almost anywhere in the world.

Sometimes in Korea, we were paid for our performance, too. We earned a bonus if we made it to the playoffs or to the finals of the mid-season tournament. I was excited about the prospect of more money, and my agent really sold it. We were paid the bonus only if we played in the games; the players on the bench missed out. So, if we were winning and it was late in the game, our coach would sub in the oldest players out of respect and let them pick up the bonus. It was impossible not to think about money as the clock was winding down.

My mother watched me play professionally for the first time in Seoul. After the game, she waited for the few straggling fans to leave with autographs and then came down from the stands smiling. She hugged me. *It's funny,* she said, squeezing my shoulders, *I forget that I'm watching you do your job—I'm just used to watching you play soccer.* Her comment reminded me of the time a new acquaintance asked me about my playing experience. *I used to play soccer, too*, she said, trying to relate. *But just for fun.*

53'

MY JOB AS A SOCCER PLAYER WAS TO WAKE UP EARLY. MY JOB
was to practice, to train, to wait. My job was to score goals. My
job was to hold my position near the final defender, to distrib-
ute the ball to my teammates. My job was to use my head. My
job was to finish, to sacrifice my body on a breakaway. My job
was to have patience, to practice good timing. My job was to run
without getting the ball, to be a decoy. My job was to yell at the
referee. My job was to watch video replays and rub Icy Hot on
my calves. My job was to rest and recover. My job was to forget.

As I got older, I noticed that soccer practice began to appeal
to me in a new way. In Seattle, training with the team but not
on a contract, I was playing with some of the best players in the
world. The environment was all pursuit and low stakes, all
improvement with no finite markers. There was an unending
feeling to practice that a game (exposition, climax, resolution)
rejected. Nothing felt more absolute, more cloistered, more limited than competition. I suppose this is what people mean when

they talk about *pressure*. To professionalize (from the Latin *prof-iteri*, to declare publicly, to profess) is to bring the weight of expectation to an activity. To play for no other reason than simple pleasure, that's amateur (from *amator*, one who loves).

In his book, Nguyen distinguishes between the purpose of playing a game and the goal of playing. He differentiates between *achievement play* and *striving play*. In achievement play, the purpose is to win. The end matters more than the means. In striving play, an individual can enjoy the game for the rewards that come from the struggle of overcoming specific obstacles. My goal was always to play professionally, to improve, to get on the field. But my purpose shifted as I grew older. No longer was I playing just to win, just to score goals. I enjoyed, for what I knew might be the last years, experiencing the beauty of this particular and fleeting expertise.

54'

BUT OF COURSE, IT'S MORE COMPLICATED THAN THAT. MONEY buys materials, focus, time. It is impossible to make art, to live, to work, without these things. Passion can act as a veil, covering up the fact that all sport is rooted in a sexist and exploitative history. When we agree to do something for free, for less than we are worth, we make ourselves, and all who aspire toward the same path, vulnerable to abuse. More recently, I saw an adapted version of the famous quote that I related to even more: *love what you do, and you will work every single day of your life.*

I remember when, before she left Norway for the World Cup, my teammate from Nigeria was sent a questionnaire from FIFA, the global governing body of soccer. In it, they asked about compensation and finances. She played for a historically underfunded national team. On the list of questions was something like: *do you think something would be lost if women's soccer players began to receive the same compensation as men?* She repeated the question to me, bemused and befuddled by its premise. If we were, we could afford a car, we could send money home, we might have savings, we might be able to do this for longer, we wouldn't need to work multiple jobs. She checked the box labeled *No* and declined the option for further comment.

55'

IN SWEDEN, ON MY SECOND PROFESSIONAL CONTRACT, I MADE
around $500 each month. After practice on the first payday, we
met with the team's manager in the equipment closet. Rows of
damp jerseys hung to dry, and a lost-and-found pile was buried
under the bottom shelf. It smelled of fresh laundry and mud. We
signed a carbon-copy receipt, and the manager handed each of the
international players a wad of fifty-Euro bills. Without counting
them, we tucked the money into our shorts as we exited the closet.
For some reason, the transaction felt illicit. The team was considered semiprofessional, so the best players, who might leave to play
on a different team, and the older, more experienced local players
were paid a small monthly stipend. Some were not paid at all. My
youngest teammates were still in high school. I knew that none
of the local girls made as much as the foreign players.

 After each payday, I returned to my apartment and stowed
one of the fifties under the floral-patterned lining of my sock
drawer, because it felt important that I come out of there with
something saved.

56'

THE TOP LEAGUE IN AUSTRALIA WAS THE W-LEAGUE (NOW known as the A-League Women). It was young (founded in 2008) and small (made up of only eight teams). The season ran for just the length of the Australian summer, which made it so players from the US could join during their offseason. The rest of the year, women in Australia played in a seven-month-long, second-tier competition. After my first season ended in the semipro league, I went to tryouts in Melbourne and Adelaide, where I hoped to secure a full-time professional contract in the W-League. In Australia, women were still paid very little, some not at all. Cole had graduated from college and was living with me when I was offered a spot on the fully professional team in Melbourne. He reminded me again of the NCAA commercial: *ninety-eight percent of college athletes will go pro in something other than sports.* This time, he meant: it's a miracle.

After our first practice in a Melbourne suburb, we were emailed PDFs of our contracts. But throughout the preseason, the coaches handed out "official" paper copies to the newest team members in the parking lot like field-trip permission slips or report cards. One player dropped her contract in the weight room, and forty black-and-white pages, stamped and signed, sprawled across the floor. She got down on her knees, embarrassed, and shuffled the papers back into a pile. I perused the details of my digital copy: I would be employed for one four-month season. I would make enough money to feed myself.

Four weeks into the season, I still hadn't been handed my papers. I signed the digital copy and sent it back to the front office. After practice that day, the coach told me he was retracting his offer, the one I'd signed and mailed. Even at the highest level, women's soccer is a lawless frontier. *So*, I thought to myself, *I will learn to be an outlaw*. I told the coach several times that I intended to fulfill my end of the contract, as, legally, he was also obligated to do. Dry mouthed and angry, he stuttered and began to mumble insults. He offered to buy me out, and I told him that I wanted to play. *You can't do that*, he said.

I could tell he was not used to a woman standing up to him, he was not used to dealing with a player who understood contract law. Later, a teammate, shocked at my steadfastness, said she would have just taken the money. She would have just let them buy her out and gone home. I suppose this was the first time I was asked to place a value on my participation. At that moment, it was immeasurable—nothing could have been worth giving up an opportunity to play.

57'

SOMETIMES I THOUGHT, *THIS MUST BE THE HARDEST JOB IN the world*. It was hard to pack my bags on a moment's notice, hard to quit jobs without warning. It was hard to leave family, leave my boyfriend, leave home, leave city after city trying to find a better team. Hard to handle bad agents, bad coaches, bad games. Hard to get out of slumps, to believe that it mattered. It was hard to care about passing the ball with myself at six a.m. before my offseason job. Language barriers were hard, injuries were hard. It was hard to meet the eye of people who told me they were surprised I was still playing, hard to say my own age aloud to myself as it crept ever higher. Twenty-four, twenty-five, twenty-six. It was hard to set my feet on the floor in the morning and, after easing weight onto tender joints, take another step. It was hard to imagine who I would be when this was all over.

58'

WHEN I WAS TWELVE YEARS OLD, THE DEFENDER ON AN OP-
posing team held on to my arm for an entire game, dragging
me away from the play. She pinched her thumb and forefinger
around my biceps and tugged on my wrist. When I went to move,
I was restrained. The fact that no one noticed, that the referee
didn't penalize the player, drove me to tears. After the game, I
remember a coach telling me that I shouldn't let other players
get in my head. I needed to learn to ignore unfairness, to let go
of what I couldn't control.

In *Flow*, Csikszentmihalyi writes that rules *facilitate concentration and involvement by making the activity as distinct as possible from the so-called "paramount reality" of everyday existence.* The
pageantry of sports, the songs and anthems, the stadiums, the
uniforms and the rules, ensure that competition is experienced
as a world apart. *For the duration of the event*, Csikszentmihalyi
writes, *players and spectators cease to act in terms of common sense,
and concentrate instead on the particular reality of the game.*

This is probably why some players—Zinedine Zidane (head-butt), Luis Suárez (biting), Diego Maradona (the Hand of God)—are often remembered for their on-field infractions. When a player breaks a rule, our understanding of the game, of its place in the world, is violently altered.

I've never thought of myself as an angry person, but I could be overcome on the field. I'm thinking, in particular, of a series of photos taken of me during a game in Sweden. In the first one, I can see the defender subtly tugging at my shorts. I lose position on the ball, and she begins to step in front of me in the second frame. By the third, I have shifted my focus away from the ball and toward her. With both of my hands, I grab her forearm. In the final photo, I am pulling her to the ground with me, grimacing with rage and effort.

I've heard the field called a stage, the game a performance. A player on the field is not the same person they are off of it. A team has characters. Some perform the most with their voices, some with their hands in big gestures, some perform with their bodies. All actors will try to bend the rules in their favor. The laws of the game are always applied unevenly. One single referee can't possibly enact them all. This is *the particular reality of the game.*

59'

SOME RULES OF THE GAME ARE DIFFICULT TO GRASP. FOR EX-
ample, unlike other sports, the offside line in soccer is not fixed,
it cannot be drawn. The "line" is an act of imagination and
changes with every step. It moves with the players. It's marked
by the body of the second-to-last defender and followed dog-
gedly by the sideline referee. Players jostle for positioning.
It's the striker's ambition to push the line forward, and the
defender's duty to hold it.

There's a scene in *Bend It Like Beckham* in which one character's mother, after much toil, finally grasps the concept of off-
sides after listening to a lesson given by her husband in which
condiments stand in for players. They cheer when she finally
declares: *the offside rule is when the French mustard has to be between the teriyaki sauce and the sea salt.*

I've tried in vain to explain the concept to befuddled friends.
Really, it's quite simple: at the moment a pass is played, there must
be two people from the opposing team between the attacker and
the goal. In some sense, the offside line emphasizes that the
striker is trying, all game, to see what she can get away with.

60'

THE LAW AGAINST HANDBALLS IS SIMPLER: WHEN THE BALL IS in play, a player must never touch it with their hands (unless they are the goalkeeper). What may sound like a constraint leads to a kind of openness, a new way of regarding certain parts of your body. Your feet become gentle and intelligent. They're able to stop a soaring ball dead, to push it just the right distance in front of you, to move alongside it. I find when I drop something now, I often catch it on the top of one foot. I've saved iPhones, mugs, take-out containers, and other fragile objects with the tips of my toes.

I've kept a photo on my desktop through all of these years. When I click on its small icon, the image enlarges, and I can see two men leaping toward the same soccer ball. They are floating in an ocean of grass, which is broken up only by the white chalk lines of a playing field. The quality of the photo is low; it was taken more than forty years ago. But still, I can discern that the two players are wearing different colors, they are on opposing teams. The attacker is a smaller man, and he is leaping higher; there is vast space between his feet and the ground. On the right edge of the photo, three defensive players are giving chase. They just barely enter the frame. Two of them are still clawing at the air as they run, desperate. One of them is standing tall, like he's just given up. The fate of the ball has been written. It's hovering only a few meters from the goal and mere inches from both the attacking forward's head and the goaltender's arm.

Maybe I love this photo because of the uncertainty of its moment. Depending on who touches it first, the ball will be tilted across the end line for a goal, or it will spill toward the defenders, who will have plenty of time to clear it away from danger.

The black-and-white still was extracted from a quarterfinal match of the men's World Cup in 1986: Argentina versus England in Mexico. The ball ended up in the goal. I didn't watch the game. I wasn't even alive on the day it was played. I didn't know the final score; I had to look it up just now: Argentina 2–1. The smaller man who is jumping is one of the most famous ever to play—Diego Maradona. He hit the ball with his fist, and it bounced once before landing in the net. After the game ended, Maradona claimed that he scored the goal *a little with the head of Maradona and a little with the hand of God.* Argentina would go on to win the World Cup.

In medieval paintings, the hand of God sometimes appears as an isolated and floating figure. It's bodiless because the depiction of God's whole person was considered sacrilegious in the Late Antique period. The historical motif is used to imply God's intervention or approval of a particular event.

I look up a video of Maradona's highlight on YouTube so I can see the moment of the photograph in context. The ball is accidentally lofted in the air, Maradona gives chase, meets with the keeper in midair, and palms the ball just out of reach. Immediately, the English players touch their arms in imitative urgency. They gesture toward the referee and insist on the handball infraction. They are furious, and they are right. They can't bear that such an important rule has been broken, that this transgression might cost them a very important game. But the referee has moved on, the goal stands.

Amidst the protesting Englishmen, Maradona can be seen sprinting to the sideline, flanked by his teammates. He jumps up in front of the fans and thrusts his fist into the air in celebration. But even in this moment, his joy is different from what we think; in an interview years later, Maradona's teammate recalled, *I could sense some doubt in his goal celebration, and he hinted at it when we embraced. He said: "To the kickoff, quick."* He must have felt tremendous relief when the referee moved the game along, when there was no longer a chance that the call would be reversed.

61'

AFTER MY CONTRACT DISPUTE, THE AUSTRALIAN COACH SWORE that he would never let me see the field. A friend and teammate who'd once played on the Australian national team tried to make me feel better. *Everyone has terrible coaches*, she told me. She described a four-year cycle: one year you will be out of form, one year you will be out of favor with the coach, one year you will be injured, and one year will go well. So, *you just have to stay in it*, she said.

During the rest of my time on the team in Australia, I had a recurring dream that I was in a wheelchair. I was on the side-lines asking why I couldn't play, trying to stand and run as my coaches and peers urged me back toward the chair. I showed them how I could walk and run in place to demonstrate my strength. Why wasn't I allowed on the field? Out of nowhere, twenty arms held my body back. Nineteen hands urged me back into the chair; one pressed down on my mouth. I would wake from the dream with a jolt, as my legs kicked my sheets off of the bed, imagining there was a soccer ball.

Each day, I caught a tram and then a train from my rented house along the Yarra River to the suburban complex where the team practiced. I played against the feeling of futility. On days when I performed well, I looked to the coach for an expression of surprise or validation. If I did what I knew I could do well, maybe I would change his mind. On days I played poorly, I looked at nothing but my own feet. Shame and frustration overwhelmed me. My teammates were distant, and I was a shell of myself, no longer animated, no longer buoyant, no longer confident. I think now of the recent reports highlighting the culture of abuse and manipulation in women's soccer, and I wonder if I would have experienced that season differently if I'd felt less alone. In the moment, all I could see was the very personal threat of a closing door.

You just have to stay in it. It's what I'd practiced my whole life. The striker's job, I thought, centers around an act of faith, plain persistence. The striker is coached to make ten runs with the hope of receiving the ball perhaps only once.

To get away from the toxic team environment, Cole and I flew up north on an off-weekend and rode in a boat out to the Great Barrier Reef. We bought the cheapest possible tickets, which meant we were on a very small boat with just enough room for fifteen people. The vessel rocked and moved with every shift in the sea. Half of the passengers were sick and took turns throwing up in the bathroom below deck. The captain cleaned up and then surfaced on the main deck to tell us that going below would make the sickness feel worse.

We were fine, and, when we arrived, they let us scuba dive without certification. Under the water, sea turtles and tropical fish swam in circles around half-bleached coral. I expected it to be calm, to be still. I associated *reef* with *beach*, but we were two hours from the shore. When I rested on the surface, I was held between massive rolling waves, and I couldn't see anything but water. For a minute, I was afraid. I felt completely alone. No team, no TV, no contracts, no agent, no coaches, no soccer. Just turtles, dead reef, and deep, deep water. Then the wave rolled back under me, and I saw the rest of the passengers floating, scattered face down in the ocean.

62'

THE SEA IN KOREA WAS CLOUDED AND BROWN. IT LOOKED DE-
void of life from where I stood on the roof of the compound. I
told myself that someday, during low tide, I would try to walk
out as far as I could, just to see how long it took me to sink into
the mud.

During the day, I watched three security guards bike in circles patrolling the area around the field and housing. Sometimes they fell asleep in the glass box where they sat near the
entrance gate. I couldn't tell if their job was to keep us in or to
protect us from something beyond the premises. I crouched
under their window as I left, so that I didn't have to explain
where I was going. It was never far—the little train that stopped
by the dorm only went back to the airport. On the way, it passed
by a few restaurants, a café, and a grocery store.

I quickly learned which guard to avoid completely, and which
one would give a benevolent wink and pass hard candies across
the desk when I bowed to him on the way to breakfast. During
my first week, the oldest guard pulled me aside on my way out

to the training field, proudly showing off the translation apps he had downloaded onto his phone. He spoke into the microphone, and his phone spoke to me: *What is your name?* I enunciated sharply, *my name is Georgia*, and he smiled as he read the transcribed Korean.

The team captain communicated important information via group text. Daily schedules and training details were distributed this way. When I ran one message through the translator before practice, it read: *I have to put the bike on my bike in the bike.* Another one: *I do not have a Santa Claus, so I think I should go to the bathroom.* At practice, the coach's yells were translated to me in calm and quiet English by my gentle translator, who stood on the sideline smiling shyly.

On my first days in the hotel during preseason, I downloaded an app and studied Hangul on my phone before I fell asleep. The writing system of the Korean language is notoriously easy to learn. It is vernacular, and was created by a fifteenth-century king with the intent of bringing literacy to the masses. I impressed my teammates by sounding out highway signs and words on the menu at dinner.

Our trainings were repetitive. Creativity gave way to rote technique and habit formation (which, in turn, gave way to creativity). Each day we began with the same possession drills, and each week we cycled through a familiar set of practices. Measures of progress were very small. The language barrier wasn't a problem once I could remember all the patterns of our passing drills. My teammates noted how quickly my confusion had subsided. But memorization, of the trainings or the alphabet, isn't the same thing as understanding.

At night and during afternoon naps, my roommate and I slept on twin beds, separated by mere feet. Her duvet was covered in a bright green-and-blue cotton fabric and mine was a light purple. When I'd arrived, I searched desperately for a cover that was closer to my familiar white cotton. I emptied cupboards in the common room while the team slept after breakfast until I found a pastel replacement.

I learned a lot about my roommate through this intimate arrangement. I soon knew she didn't drink coffee, she liked to use cosmetic face masks, she enjoyed eating candy in her bed at night. I knew she had a girlfriend who was twenty-six, I knew she liked to sleep in, and I watched as she leaned over the sink and dyed her hair from black to blond and then to black again. In the brutal heat of the summer, we lay naked across the room from each other, sprawled on our beds. But we didn't often speak. On the field, my typically vocal leadership was reduced to movements, gestures, and, often, to shouts in a language I knew my teammates couldn't understand. When I missed a shot, I could only shrug, and they could only sigh.

Even my teammates who otherwise spoke no English could say one word: *fighting*. I learned quickly that fighting could mean "stay strong," it could mean "suck it up," it could mean "chin up," it could mean "cheer up," it could mean "move on," it could mean "play hard" or "let's go!" There was a certain strength there in hiding emotion, in fighting through most things instead of for them.

In Karlskoga, my coach spoke only Swedish, which, even after a few weeks, sometimes sounded to me like Russian, sometimes Italian, sometimes German. The coach in Lithuania was almost mute; he nodded and glared with a gruff manner, and, when he was happy, he showed it with a broad, toothy smile. Everywhere I went, I found that I missed being yelled at. I wanted commands—I longed for the clarity of direction.

63'

IN KOREA, WE PLAYED OUR HOME GAMES IN A TOWN CALLED Hwacheon. The northernmost part of the city was only nine kilometers from the Demilitarized Zone, a strip of land that acts as a border barrier, a buffer zone between North and South Korea. Because of this, the majority of the population of Hwacheon was made up of soldiers. They spent their weekends in PC game rooms, ferrying bags of beer and chips from the 7-Eleven to their motels. They waved and said hello to me, practicing English and laughing as I walked by.

Our stadium was the smallest in the league. Come seven p.m., when games kicked off, young soldiers filled the grandstand. They would cheer and clap, breaking my name down into the three convenient syllables that made up the Korean spelling on the back of my jersey: *Jo-ji-ah*.

But we also played in empty arenas. A college friend who lived in Seoul came to one of my games at Hyochang Stadium, in the heart of the capital city. It had seats for just over 15,000 people. It was raining on the night this friend watched, so the usually small audience was reduced even more. Maybe fifty people were scattered in the stands, each bundled in blankets and covered by their own umbrella.

I found my friend after the game ended and they hugged me, congratulated me on the win, and then asked what it felt like to look up and see no one, to play in an empty stadium, vast and full of echo. *Does it ever feel sad?*

64'

IN SWEDEN, I SHARED AN APARTMENT WITH A ROOMMATE from Pennsylvania. We connected well on the field; our chemistry was immediate and productive. We both played forward and regularly assisted each other's goals. On alternate weeks, our photos would adorn the front page of the small town's newspaper. In some of them, we were pictured in an ecstatic, post-goal embrace. On the bus after our away games, we came alive to each other, sharing insight and analysis. *We should have played in a 4-3-3, we should have saved a substitute for later, the gaps were too big, our press too low.* An accelerated intimacy arises from collective ambition. No matter where I played, my name on the field was shortened from Georgia to George to the intimate, tender *G*.

But off the field, my roommate and I had little in common. We spent many of our days walking circles around each other in our small kitchen and talking to our families on FaceTime behind the closed doors of our bedrooms, where windows framed perfect squares of dense pine forest. She laughed with loving bewilderment at my compulsive reading, and I rolled my eyes at her addiction to Netflix.

It was the same on almost every team I played. The ease and comfort of goal-oriented communication fell away when the game ended. The relationship shifted when we arrived home after practice, tired and sore. At most, my teammates and I shared a sense of humor, an ambition, and a refined skill. We shared the simple fact of finding ourselves working in a country where we could speak fluently to very few people. I often found myself longing for a connection that endured beyond the confines of the field, that I could tie into my life past a single shared season.

On the other hand, when I spoke to my closest friends back home, I had to limit conversations about soccer to the game's most elementary components: happy, sad, winning, losing.

65'

IN HIS MEMOIR, *OPEN*, ANDRE AGASSI WRITES THAT PLAYING tennis is like being on an island. *Of all the games men and women play, tennis is the closest to solitary confinement.* I've heard other famous biographers argue the same about boxing and swimming, both individual sports, both so obvious in their loneliness. The same is often said about the practice of writing, in which an artist is confined to the world of her mind. Marguerite Duras once wrote, *the person who writes books must always be enveloped by a separation from others.*

In *The Lonely Goalkeeper*, an op-doc produced by *The New York Times*, former Arsenal legend Bob Wilson speaks about the feeling of being an outsider on the soccer field. He often felt like he was *the only individual in what is a team game*, and said there was *an incredible loneliness about it.* The goalkeeper is the most obviously isolated player on the soccer field. But if you watch a striker celebrate a goal, you might notice that it's also a lonely act, an impulsively solitary run. Strikers sprint away from their team. They run down the goal line, arms outstretched, head back, eyes closed. Perhaps they will shout, jump, slide, but their first instinct is always to move away. No one can touch them, because, for a moment, they don't want to be touched.

Some spread their arms into wings. Some praise God, crossing their chest, and others slide, wet turf ferrying them toward their fans. Most often, I dropped to my knees and pumped my fists in the air. Cristiano Ronaldo's celebration might be the most famous of all. I've seen children mimic it, seen silhouetted images of his broad stance painted on walls across Europe. Ronaldo runs, jumps, turns in the air, and plants, feet wide and arms pointed toward the ground in a reverent ritual to his own body. Against Atlético Madrid, Ronaldo scores in the final minutes to win. His teammates are quick to surround their star. They mob him, reaching for hugs and kisses. Still, even here, he jumps up, shaking them off as he rises to complete this gesture to himself.

Werner Herzog's documentary *The Great Ecstasy of Woodcarver Steiner* follows a ski jumper's quest for the world record in 1974. In each of his jumps, the titular Steiner far exceeds his competitors. He is in a league of his own. The movie ends with an image of Steiner skiing away from the base of a jump after a triumphant climax—he has broken the world record; he has landed safely. He is alone, surrounded by nothing but the blank whiteness of snow.

Across the screen, we see words adapted from Robert Walser's "Helblings Geschichte": *I should be all alone in this world. I, Steiner, and no other living being. No sun, no culture, I, naked on a high rock, no storm, no snow, no streets, no banks, no money, no time and no breath. Then I wouldn't be afraid anymore.*

66'

IN *THE WAVES*, PERCIVAL IS AN OBJECT OF FANTASY AND PRO-
jection. The protagonists are infatuated, but they don't want to
be Percival. It would be nice to live like him, Neville says, *But
I cannot stand all day in the sun with my eyes on the ball; I cannot
feel the flight of the ball through my body and think only of the ball.*
Neville watches Percival play cricket after school from the safety
of a grassy knoll. He looks down on Percival as the brute rolls
in the grass, chews on a wheat stalk, and is trailed by a flock of
young boys. Neville is a pining lover, a close observer, a fan,
and this affords him proximity to joy, to pain, to the physical-
ity of Percival. But he doesn't have to sacrifice his own life.

David Foster Wallace writes that athletes *give themselves over
to a pursuit . . . and enjoy a relationship to perfection that we admire
and reward . . . and love to watch even though we have no inclina-
tion to walk that road ourselves. In other words,* he explains, *they
do it "for" us, sacrifice themselves for our (we imagine) redemption.*

I recently watched a documentary about a blind man who
spent twenty-one days kayaking on the Colorado River through

the Grand Canyon. The viewer watches as he wakes up each morning to the roar of the whitewater that he (with the help of guides) will have to navigate blindly. He never smiles when the camera is focused on him. Instead, he is frozen in seriousness and seems to be in a constant state of stress. He explains that he hates when people tell him anything is possible. *Barriers are real*, he says to the camera. *They are solid things, and they hurt.* Still, in the end, he climbs back up the riverside to float down a rapid that bested him, just so he can say he really did the whole thing.

Wallace continues: Tracey Austin's autobiography *could have been about both the seductive immortality of competitive success and the less seductive but way more significant fragility and imperma-nence of all the competitive venues in which mortal humans chase immortality.* Yes, aren't I concerned with making something that lasts?

But a belief in immortality is only available to the spectator. Halls of fame and records and medals and posters are most meaningful to fans. The job of the athlete is not to mythologize her own life. Instead, she confronts mortality directly, unavoid-ably. The job of the athlete is to navigate unrelenting decay.

67'

IN AN ARTICLE FOR *THE NEW YORK TIMES*, SAM ANDERSON writes about the common compulsion to watch and rewatch videos of horrendous sports injuries. He describes the sports fan as someone who wants to *travel to distant realms of exhaustion, urgency, terror and joy* they themself cannot access. Anderson describes athletes as *experiential astronauts*. They get to see what most people don't, and they will define the limits of our existence.

I watch compilation videos online: *Worst Sports Injuries 2018–2019, Most Devastating Injuries of All Time*. Kevin Durant's Achilles, Gordon Hayward's broken leg, Kurt Zouma's ACL tear. The videos have millions of views. Anderson's theory about the sports fan's fascination with these images, their enjoyment of them, is that a spectator wants to see the athlete *come into contact with the real*. They want to know that *the high drama of sport—that spectacle of humans going right up to the edge of possibility—is not just a meaningless distraction*. It has physical stakes, it has consequences.

68'

ONCE, IN AN EFFORT TO LOCATE THE EXACT SOURCE OF MY
back pain, I drove with my translator to get scans at a hospital
in Seoul. First, they took an X-ray, and we all looked at it together on the wall. The doctor slid the scan onto a backlit dis-
play. There were fake plants on either side of the screen. She
told me my spine was a bit bent; I saw how it moved from left
to right like a snake. She told me my neck was permanently
arched forward from too much reading or looking down (for
weeks after this, I held my books above me while I lay flat on
my back, believing I could unfold myself like a piece of paper).
These were new problems, ones I didn't know I had, and also,
they were irrelevant to the nerve pain radiating down my leg.
In the picture, the three of us could also see my plastic IUD and
the Apple headphones I'd forgotten to take out of my pocket,
a tangled mess of wire.

Before the last game of the season, I walked to a hospital
next to our hotel with the team doctor. I'd been told I needed
to play in the game that night. A win would secure our spot in

the playoffs. The doctor (we called her "Doctor") spoke in Korean with the attendant as she pulled a clear liquid into two syringes. I didn't ask what was in the shots. I got one in each hip. The effects of the medicine would last for about three hours, Doctor told me, just until the end of the game. The shots weren't covered by my insurance, so I had to pay for them with cash. The visit cost me seven dollars.

After the injections, I played in a state of numbness. I felt nothing at all in my lower back. I was slightly dizzy, drunk on the feeling of being pain-free for the first time in weeks. I scored three goals and didn't remember any of them until watching a recording of the game the next day with the team in the meeting room back at the compound. Coach stopped and slowed the footage, rewound and showed all of the goals as he smiled in my direction. My teammates turned toward me, clapping, and I had a familiar feeling of dissociation. Was it me on that screen?

But I did remember Doctor giving me a thumbs up from the sideline, and I remember returning her gesture with a wide smile. After the game, she had leaned toward me with a cupped hand at the side of her mouth and whispered excitedly: *Korean injections are good, aren't they?*

69'

I EXPERIENCED A SIMILAR FEELING OF DISSOCIATION AFTER an appointment with a podiatrist in Minnesota. *Most of my patients*, the doctor explained, *have had very good results.* Maybe a 95 percent success rate, he estimated. *Though*, he admitted, *one did come back saying that he felt like he no longer knew what his body was.*

We were somewhere off the highway in a cold, dry, snowed-in suburb. Mine was the only car in the parking lot. I was there because I wanted to get nerve-killing chemicals injected into my right foot; a ball of tissue had grown around the nerve between my third and fourth toe, and the squeeze of my tight cleats was unbearable. The doctor's office was bare. I had no insurance between seasons, and I tried not to think about how much the injections were going to cost me. But I knew it didn't matter. I would do what was needed so that I could play. At all costs.

There were times I think I would have died on the field, would have died to play soccer. Playing made the present moment so expansive, so immersive that, in the *particular reality of the game*, even as it touched up against the actual reality of the rest of my life, I would have given anything to continue.

The doctor walked into the room without a knock. He had an ashen smear on his forehead, and I confirmed it was a Wednesday. His movements made me feel like I was in a sports movie. Maybe this was the scene where the athlete makes a bad decision about drugs or friends or her future. His back was turned to me as he filled up a syringe and flicked the tip of its needle with his middle finger. He was wearing slippers. It felt pleasing to have such agency, to be reckless in the treatment of my own body, to rebel against its preservation, to give something up. The feeling of fire consumed my toes, then the feeling of nothing.

70'

SOMETIMES I THINK OF MY BODY AS AN OBJECT; I THINK OF ALL the things I have done to it. Worn tight-fitting cleats, headed the ball, slept on my stomach, ran without stretching. I think of the various pains I know well. I know what it is like to be kicked in the shin, I know the ache of a bruised toenail, the throb of the one that is poised to fall off; I know the feeling of a cleat sliding down the inside of my thigh, an elbow to the cheekbone, the willing split of skin; I know the feeling of falling straight onto frozen ground, of two heads colliding at the temple, I know the dull buzz of a brain contusion; I know the sensation of dehydration, of a hamstring cramping, its involuntary flexion.

After games and practices in Korea, we were invited to soak at the local bathhouse, or jjimjilbang. The sting and tingle of the hot water could eliminate small pains, temporarily.

The first time I went, I followed my teammate Boram, who instructed me to bring my own shampoo and soap. The rest of the team had already begun their post-training soak, and they

were scattered in pools filled with water of various tempera-
tures. They walked back and forth from the hot to the cold,
soaking their sore and tired limbs. A young girl I didn't know
held the arm of her mother, and they traversed the tiled floor
of the bathroom. I watched Boram and another woman walk
together toward the hot bath. Boram was thirty years old. She
was rail thin, strong, lean, nothing extra on her. In one swift
movement, the two of them bent in synchrony and filled plastic buckets full of water. They returned to their stools, soaped
and scrubbed their garments, and then left them to soak as they
began their own shower.

I was too big for the jjimjilbang. If I didn't sit on a stool,
I had to bend awkwardly to fit under a showerhead. When I
did sit, my knees—gangly, dangerous things—entered into my
neighbor's washing territory. I was pink, a unique hue, after
soaking in the hot water. When I left to dry off, I discovered
that the towels at the sauna were miniature, too small to cover
me. I watched my naked body move in the mirrors while my
teammates stood nearby blow-drying their hair and mois-
turizing meticulously. I came from a family of chicken legs
and dancers, but my body had been shaped by and for sprinting and kicking. My legs were out of proportion. At my stron-
gest, I sensed that my thighs were tree trunks, my calves, strong
branches. I planted my feet on the ground with a firm rooted-
ness. I felt thick, weighted, unmovable.

71'

OTHER TIMES, I CONSIDERED MY BODY AS A SUBJECT, AS ITS own actor. I tried to listen to what it wanted and negotiate some of my own desires. Some nights, I wanted to stay up late, and my body, tired, dragged me into a deep sleep.

In the waiting room at a different hospital back home in the States, the TV was on mute. They were airing a memorial for Dale Earnhardt. Even without the sound, I learned a lot about him—he was a NASCAR driver, and that day was the anniversary of his death. I recognized the name, but when I googled him, I realized there were two: a Junior and a Senior. I wasn't sure which one I knew of. In my search, I found a video of the crash in which the older man had died. It was very gruesome. When I looked up at the TV again, the Junior was there, racing laps, doing the same thing that killed his father.

I was at the hospital to meet with a sports medicine doctor about the torn cartilage in my knee. I told him I had to play the next week, I was supposed to be on a plane in the morning. I just needed the pain to subside for a few months while I played out a short contract in Norway. Syringe in hand, the doctor asked, *do you want to be able to crouch down, to be able to pick up your grandchildren?* I shook my head, said *no*, told him *I don't care.* My body communicated through pain. In a betrayal, I ignored its request for rest, and the doctor gave me what I asked for.

The meniscus is the viscous barrier between your shin bone and femur. Torn, it's known to flip and catch, to move up and down. I've been told by several doctors and experienced friends that the cartilage might rest flatly and painlessly, or it might fold over itself and agitate. For two years after these injections, the knee didn't bother me at all. It was behaving, it was permissive. It allowed me a day, a week, and then a season of pain-free play. Still, it was hard for me not to worry about when the injury might change its mind.

For the most part, the hurt complied with my wishes. It stayed buried in the small pocket of flesh under my kneecap. It was an injury being born. But eventually, the slight swell of the tissue pushed against the inside of my jeans, felt just different enough when I walked. The feeling was more distraction than pain; I was haunted by the idea of its progress.

72'

THERE WERE SO MANY DOCTOR'S OFFICES, THERE WERE TRAINing rooms, there were ACE bandages and ice packs. There was always an ailment, always an awareness of the body's fragility. It smelled like stale ice, like old water, like hot packs ready to warm a big muscle. After practice in Korea, we all filed into the training room where we were comforted by compression pants, massages, needles, pebbles to walk on, pills, and other experimental treatments.

After I injured the disc in my back, I made subtle accommodations to maneuver around the pain, because the only other option was to succumb to it. I watched a YouTube video intended for geriatric patients and learned to put my socks on with my back flat on my bed, legs raised above me. When I bent down to pick something up, I squatted deeply, legs butterflied, or brought myself down to my knees. When in pain, it is hard to remember the moments when the body has felt like a convenient tool, an object which we deftly control. When it is comfortable, the body can be set aside, rested, and enjoyed for its competence and skill. When irritated, it is an interruption. I become all body and no mind.

July 7, 2016, Incheon: I am too tired to write, there is nothing in my brain.

73'

MOST OFTEN, AN ATHLETE DOESN'T CHOOSE WHEN TO RETIRE. They don't quit at a high point. Their body wears down, or their athleticism and talent erode. But no matter the circumstance, the thing that has given a life its shape comes to a close.

Women athletes confront another ending: the prime age for athletic competition can coincide and overlap with the only window for childbirth.

I can still see Boram walking into my room mid-season. She held a bundle of brightly colored elastic headbands in front of her as she approached. Her eyes were downcast; she looked embarrassed. She had been sidelined on and off for a month with stomach pain. She hadn't been able to travel or to practice with us. My curtains were open, and the room was harshly illuminated by the light reflecting off the bay. Boram pulled the windows closed. In broken English, she told me she was pregnant. I could see tears collecting, threatening to fall. She sat on the end of my twin bed. I knew she had dreams of playing for the national team again, and this would set her back another year, at least. She was almost thirty. Before she left my room, she handed me her headbands and said she wouldn't need them anymore.

74'

AT MY MOM'S HOUSE ON A BREAK BETWEEN SEASONS, I HOB-
bled around the kitchen, searching for a remedy for my constant foot pain and my sore knees. I was pressed up against the
limit of my body, I could feel its sharp perimeter, its cold edges.
I sifted through medicine cabinets and junk drawers, swal-
lowed fistfuls of ibuprofen, washed them down with a beer. A
pastel drawing of mine from childhood hung above the stove:
a house, a girl, and a dog. *Life is long, Georgia*, said my sixty-
year-old mother. She was coaxing me to retire, to move on to
a pursuit that wouldn't disintegrate my body with such persistent logic. I wanted to cry. My soccer life felt so short. Because
it *was* so short.

Open begins at the end of Andre Agassi's career. In the first
scene, Agassi is preparing to compete in his last professional
tennis tournament. Agassi describes a *second death* the athlete
experiences as they near retirement. *If tennis is life*, he writes,
then what follows tennis must be the unknowable void. He is in ex-

cruciating pain and wakes up in a haze of disassociation. *Please let this be over,* he thinks as he struggles out of bed. And then he contradicts himself: *I'm not ready for it to be over.*

The voice in my head—*what else? and what next?*—increased in volume and urgency each year I played. At the end of every season, teetering on the edge of this unknowable void, I wondered if I would ever put on a jersey again.

I didn't tell Boram I wanted children someday. I didn't tell her I thought of motherhood as an end to my playing, even though I know plenty of women who returned to the field after giving birth. It seemed too difficult. With the clock perpetually winding down on my career, a pregnancy seemed like an unnecessary injury. It meant the sacrifice of an entire year, or more. I always considered parenthood a phase of life that would come after. When she left my room, I held her headbands: pink, blue, black, gray. I rolled their sticky rubber between my fingers, slid the blue one over my baby hairs, and wondered how much longer I had to spare.

When I asked myself why I was still playing, I had trouble answering. The truest thing I could think of was: joy. I still loved the high feeling of scoring, the sense of touch, the leather-on-leather feel of ball to shoe, the familiar smell of mud mixed with sweat, of hot rubber turf, the exhaustion, the slippery feeling of playing through summer thunderstorms. But I did sometimes wonder if my joy was enough.

I kept a mental list of things I would do when I finished

playing soccer: start long-distance running, prioritize writing, tend to a garden, take cello lessons, cut my hair so short it didn't fit in a ponytail, have babies.

A couple years after I left Korea, I turned the TV on to watch South Korea play against Australia in the Women's World Cup. I saw Boram standing strong on the back line. She was commanding and strong. She cleared the ball with confidence and slide-tackled attackers with wonderful grace and timing. As I watched, I realized I was just as old as she was the day she'd cried on the edge of my bed. Her one-year-old daughter was somewhere in the stands sitting with her father. Korea defended well, and the game ended in a draw.

75'

WHEN SEVENTY-FIVE MINUTES HAVE PASSED, THE CLOCK TILTS toward finality. We will make the last adjustments and substitutions. Fatigue will shape what we are capable of accomplishing. Our abilities have been hoarded in preparation for what might finally be demanded of them. Maybe just one more sprint, one final effort. As the game progresses, mental focus makes up for tired muscles and bones. We practice for this. We are ready. If the weather is cold, we are warmed past the point of sensing the wind. If the weather is warm, we are slicked in damp coolness. With just fifteen minutes left, the passage of time flattens all elements to simply: the environment of the game. We don't have to last much longer.

76'

A YEAR BEFORE I FINALLY QUIT, I WAS CALLED INTO A MEETING with the coach in his basement office at Memorial Stadium. Just three weeks prior, I'd been invited to preseason with the professional team in Seattle after playing well at an open tryout. The field was ancient, its facilities were crumbling. Behind the coach's head was all exposed plumbing and unpainted cement. He was sorry, but I would be one of the last players cut from the preseason roster.

As ever, there was a sense that it might end there. I felt the bloom of regret; soccer was a flooded stream, damp and borderless. My uniform from last night's game was still sloshing in circles in the wash, and I could hear the machines rumbling in the room next door. I shook the coach's hand and walked, stunned, into the laundry room. This was how quickly things came and went.

The equipment manager waved as he left for lunch and said he would catch me tomorrow. I nodded my head, even though I knew I would probably never see him again. I watched the laundry going around and around. I said goodbye to my sports bra and socks. I grabbed my backpack and left without the rest. There was no reason to wait.

This is all part of your journey, my trainer texted me after he heard the news. *Let me know when you are ready to work on what's next*. I wondered where he thought I was going. And if he knew, I wished he would just tell me.

77'

AFTER I FAILED TO SECURE A CONTRACT IN SEATTLE, I SIGNED a three-month deal to compete for a Lithuanian club in the UEFA Champions League, which features the top clubs from each European country. The short contract was a way to keep playing during the gap between this season and the next. The Lithuanian team had acquired three Americans to help boost its chances in the international competition. We all lived together five blocks from the training field.

On the first night, I arrived at two a.m. and knocked on the door of the old brick house until my new roommate appeared at its threshold, bleary eyed, to let me in. My bag had been lost on my trip to Lithuania, so I foraged in the closet and drawers of the bedroom I'd been given. There were soccer socks, training tops, shorts, and a faux-fur coat hanging in the closet, which I would wear with irony when my housemates and I went to the movies. All of it was evidence of the players who had come and gone, just like I would, passing through. A king bed took up most of the room. I lay across it, sprawled and exhausted. I felt as though I had stepped into someone else's life.

At the first training, desperate for me to join the team, the head coach brought a bucket of old cleats. I tried on the shoes; each pair was either narrow and uncomfortable or too big and impossible to wear. I trained in running shoes and, after practice, the manager brought me to a half-abandoned mall, where I picked out a cheap pair to get me through the week.

78'

WHEN I FIRST CONTEMPLATED THE OFFER TO COME TO LITH-
uania, I hummed to myself the song that plays before every
men's Champions League game. The anthem begins with an
orchestral crescendo and builds to a chorus of voices singing,
in various languages:

> *The Masters,*
> *The Best,*
> *The big teams*
> *The champions*

I pictured myself lined up in the middle of the field before
a game, closing my eyes, throwing my head skyward and listening.

We played our first Women's Champions League game at
home against a team from Prague. As we walked out to midfield before the game, I was surprised to hear no music playing.
(In 2021, the women's league did finally compose an anthem,

but it sounded to me like an imitation, a lesser companion to one we already knew). Instead, a familiar quiet filled the stadium. All we had was our focus, our selves.

The female athlete arrived late to the scene, again and again. It had already been built by the time she joined: the stadiums, the statues, the uniforms, the rules to the game, the anthems. Marathons had been run; mountains already climbed by men. The female athlete was confined to this space, asked to define herself against a given vocabulary.

79'

AND IT IS THE ATHLETE'S OBLIGATION TO TURN SUFFERING INTO
something good. She needs to carry stories with her about coming up against obstructions, overcoming them, and being stronger for it. Supposedly we are all on a *journey*. When something changes, it's the start of the *next chapter* or a *new beginning*. When I am asked about my experiences playing professionally, I have a few practiced lines to share. I speak to friends, interviewers, strangers, all the same. The story is flat, easy to live with. After a while, I began to think it might be true. *I had a lot of fun. I got to travel the world. I was out of my comfort zone. So much great food, beautiful cities, unique culture. Do something you love, and you will never work a day in your life.* An athletic career could have the arc of a story. But an entire life nests in this arc.

The mythic Hero's Journey begins in the known world and moves toward the unknown. In an essential part of his travels, the hero encounters tests and hardships, often in groups of three. Joseph Campbell explains: *The original departure into the land of trials represented only the beginning of the long and really perilous path of initiatory conquests and moments of illumination. Dragons have now to be slain and surprising barriers passed—again, again, and again.* The journey is one of setbacks and triumphs and, ultimately, a return. Campbell, incidentally, was also an athlete, an elite runner. For a time, he was one of the fastest half-mile runners in the world.

I once tried to write thinly veiled fiction about success and failure, about aging, about sports. An editor responded to a story of mine, saying: *Thanks for sending your story, "The Tennis Player," which is quite a convincing portrait of a player at the end of his career. We have a couple of such stories in the issue already and they tend to go somewhat deeper into the psychology of rising and falling from the top of a sport.* I knew that part of the problem was that my character never fell. The story was colored by a slow fade; it was boredom, it was easing on the brakes, it was ambivalence. I couldn't avoid writing the truth of my life into its pages; there had been no fall, no climax, no clean ending. It makes for bad fiction.

Tracey Austin's book fails, Wallace argues, in part because of the simplicity of its language. Triumphs and tragedies are written in staccato, robotic diction and devoid of any true human feeling. The reader wants in on the emotional highs and, especially, the lows. The non-athlete reader craves the drama of sharp triumphs and tragedies, not a dulled-down tale of strong-willed determination.

In *A Body, Undone*, Christina Crosby writes against the idea of the Hero's Journey. Her book is a memoir of her body, which was transformed dramatically from able-bodied to quadriplegic after a bike accident. *Whatever chance I have at a good life, in all senses of that phrase, depends on my openness to the undoing wrought by spinal cord injury, because there is no return to an earlier life.* Typical narratives of suffering, disability, or pain, she writes, carry *the troubled subject through painful trials to livable accommodations and lessons learned, and all too often sound the note triumphant. Don't believe it.* Instead of a return, there is perpetual and permanent change. In other words, the truth of life is less like a chapter and more like an endlessly unfurling scroll.

80'

RECENTLY, I WENT TO SEE A NEW DOCTOR ABOUT THE KNEE that still bothers me. He told me, *injections like the ones you were given can cause damage. Many doctors would refuse to administer those to someone your age.* I nodded. I did know this, do know this. *I am a different person now,* I assured him, laughing. I tried to maintain my respect for this former self while demonstrating a newfound maturity. I was retired. I had all the time in the world to treat my injury, to heal. *But back then,* I told him as a means of explanation, *I had to play.* I could hear his patience wearing thin when he replied: *and many sports medicine doctors would agree that there is no such thing in this world as "had to play."*

Soccer is a flat slab of stone, a sheet of slate I have to bend my knees in order to lift. It occurs to me that I might still be discovering the extent of my sacrifice. I am still trying to teach my body I can be kind; I know and respect its limits; I want to live a long life inside of it.

But I know that hasn't always been true. I remember getting a concussion in high school, another in college, another at some point that I chose to ignore so I didn't have to miss a game. Eventually, I stopped counting because they were very hard to tally. The pain was unlike a broken bone; it was immeasurable and invisible. The feeling was all vagueness and blur.

Some research says that even the repetition of heading the ball, a relatively gentle blow when compared to contact with an elbow or another skull, might cause long-term damage. My grandfather, a retired neuroscientist, urged me to stop playing until the day he died. His whole life, he kept a brain in a bucket in his closet, another one sliced and preserved in sheets of glass on his coffee table. He pointed them out whenever I came over, lifting the lid to reveal the smell of formaldehyde. *You only get one!* He'd tell me. But there is a difference between what our minds know and what our bodies compel us to do.

81'

PHENOMENOLOGISTS USE THE CONCEPTS OF *BODY IMAGE* AND *body schema* to describe the way we picture ourselves in space. If you were to wear a blindfold, the body schema would enable you still to locate and identify parts of your body, to find your own nose in the dark. The body schema is the network of knowledge that enables movement and reaction. In sports, a schema is shaped by practice and repetition.

Watching baseball, I marvel at the speed of the batter's decision making. I read somewhere online that batters have only 0.25 seconds after a pitch is thrown to decide whether or not to swing. That fact makes a hit seem impossible, and, at first, I assume they must be relying on chance, hoping to get lucky when they swing. But then I remember these players have practiced every day, for years, for this very moment. It strikes me that they know exactly what they are doing. The movement is a part of them; their body can perform it without the help of their conscious, thinking brain. They are all action.

Elite athletes can also develop something called *the yips*, whereby the subtle craft of a tennis serve, a golf putt, a baseball pitch, a back handspring, is suddenly lost, sometimes forever. No one can agree on a cause or determine whether the condition is neurological or psychological. The dictionary calls it *a state of nervous tension*. But the symptoms are consistent: a once-familiar motion is suddenly alien.

I still find myself waking with a jolt from the recurring dream in which I am trying to sprint across a soccer field but my legs are moving in slow motion. I often wonder what physical knowledge is dissipating, has already left me. Will I be able to sense when my body has been wiped clean of its efforts?

Christina Crosby writes, *I don't want to forget how those pleasures felt in my body, and I fear the erosion of embodied memory.*

I map the history of my own body by its scars. Right knee: Minneapolis, 2014, surgery, three half-inch incisions. Right cheekbone: Melbourne, 2015, elbow, three stitches. Right ring finger: Minneapolis, 2012, avocado and knife. Left tibia: Portland, cleat mark, three inches.

82'

I'VE TRIED TO FINISH THE STORY OF SOCCER BEFORE. WHEN college was ending, I wrote in an article for the school paper: *After four years in a Division III program, I have learned to love soccer in small-sided games with strangers, in its facilitation of conversation, in its ability to empower women, and in the universality of the game.*

And then I rewrote the same story years later in a different essay, with the added commentary: *I knew when I wrote it that I didn't believe it, but I hoped that by writing it, I might start to. For the first time, I thought I had played my last game. I had no other way to cope with the devastating realization that I might never compete again after college. Soccer needed to fit into a different narrative, one in which it had passed.*

This was closer to the truth, but it still wasn't true. What am I circling around? The process of writing is iterative and unending. Revision and ambition coalesce to make success feel illusive and ill-defined. In an essay for *The New York Times*, Rachel Cusk compares writing to mountaineering. *Writing [was] a story of endeavor, of lonely mountain-climbing, of pitting oneself against things that no one else seemed much troubled by,* she writes. *The search for consummation, for an ending, only seemed to create the necessity for beginning again. . . . I had gone away from the world . . . further and further away in pursuit of finality, of an ending, without, it seemed, considering how I was going to get back.*

In *The White Dress,* Nathalie Léger depicts the famous New York Yankee Mickey Mantle's struggles to write about baseball in his autobiography: *How to describe the trajectory of a baseball?* She summarizes from his perspective: *I wanted to describe . . . the air, the rustling air, the space—the hole the ball makes against the background, its shape and how it has warped by the time it reaches me, its exact line when it takes off again, that I conceive in my mind a millisecond before I hit it, afterward I don't look at it any longer, I've already gone, I'm not looking at it but I keep an eye on it, that's something else—that's what I wanted to tell.*

Instead of a beginning, middle, and end, I want to describe the touch of a soccer ball against the leather grain of a cleat. I want to describe the feeling of the perfect strike, which will inevitably carry the ball on an arc past the goalkeeper's out-stretched hands. I want to describe the feeling you get when you let go of a perfect pass, its weight leaving the foot, all tension, inertia, and backspin. Yes, it is a hole against a background of repetition, experience, love.

83'

IT IS JUNE, AND IT HAS BEEN YEARS SINCE I STOPPED PLAYING, but I still wake up at five a.m., before my summer job working for the parks department, to run sprints up the hill by my house. Fast-twitch muscles are responsible for the short bursts of energy and power employed during jumping, sprinting, and lifting weights. After a week of inactivity, it is said, they are reduced by 15 percent. My thighs shrink without the everyday effort of jostling for position on the field. As you age, you lose fast-twitch muscles at a much higher rate than slow-twitch, the muscles for long-distance running and endurance-related activities. I was a moderately skilled player. But more than anything, I was fast. I think often about the fact that fast is what goes first.

On a morning run, I pass an older couple. As I jog by, my headphones in my ears with no music playing, I overhear the woman say *those are beautiful legs*, as though I am an animal, a horse, a dog. I have taken myself out for a walk. I wag my tail and bark. When I come in for breakfast looking exhausted, Cole compliments my strength and resilience before telling me gently, *you know you don't have to do that anymore.*

An old agent of mine calls while I am cleaning the drains at the city pool. Mud has built up over years, and I am grabbing at families of worms and green frogs with gloved hands. Hair, pine needles, plastic bits. My stomach lurches with anticipation and dread. I contemplate ignoring the call, putting the phone back in my pocket. But before the ringing stops, I take off one glove and pick up. Maybe it's habit that compels me to answer, maybe vocation.

The agent says he is just calling to catch up. He is building a new house for his family in the Swedish countryside. I've known him for so long that, in some ways, he feels like a friend. *Are you still playing?* he asks. And I don't know why, but I feel a sudden embarrassment. *Yes*, I tell him, even though it has been a long time since I've played competitively. I didn't make a retirement announcement; I hadn't posted a photo montage of my career or said thank you to my teammates and coaches. I'd opted, instead, for an indefinite hiatus. I imagined I was keeping a door open for myself; I couldn't help but place a finger between the threshold and its latch.

The feeling I have on the phone call comes close to the panic I feel when I read of Anne Boyer's fear in *The Undying*: that I "had devoted my life to writing and sacrificed all that I had to never come to its reward."

Wherever I turned, I ran into soccer, bruised my hips on its sharp edges. I still struggle to pass by a ball lying idly in a grassy lawn, or one that has come to rest in the corner of my living room. I can't help but roll it toward me, lift it up with my toes, cradle it on the crown of my foot, and balance it there for a moment.

Our team in Australia arranged for a speaker to talk to the team about leadership. He was a retired football player. He dressed in business clothes: a navy sweater, leather shoes, and slacks. His body still pulled tightly at the seams and gave the impression of strength. I only remember one thing he said to us. I think of the words often: *remember that who you are is separate from what you do.*

84'

PARTWAY THROUGH GRADUATE SCHOOL, I TOOK A JOB COACH-
ing soccer at a liberal arts college two hours away. Every week,
I drove back and forth between worlds. The road wound through
monotonous wheat fields. I listened to *The New Yorker: Fiction*
podcasts and recorded voice memos of my stories for class to
transcribe later. I wrote a lot in the car, and I was back to the
old habit of movement propelled by restlessness. Maybe my
mind delighted in it as much as my body once had.

At my new job, I made friends with a librarian. *I must admit*,
she told me, *you have a bit of a reputation at the library. Who is
the soccer coach*, they'd all been wondering, *who reads so many
books?*

A girl who can write like this ought not worry about goal
kicks. *I was wrong when I said that*, the teacher told me years
later. *The reason you can write like that is* because *you worry about
the goal kicks.*

85'

EVERY YEAR I TOLD MYSELF I WOULD PLAY JUST ONE MORE
season—I would play until I stopped enjoying it. It made me
sad, the idea that my pleasure could be used up, like my body
or time. But the joy never did dry up. Instead, by the time I
landed in Norway, I had applied to graduate school on a whim,
and, for the first time, I was making plans for my future that
didn't revolve around soccer. On free mornings or rest days, I
left my napping teammates and took the train from our town,
traveling twenty minutes through a long tunnel into Bergen.
I loved the city, its dark bars and cafés, its universities, its min-
imalist restaurants, and the clothing stores filled with sleek
Scandinavian designs I couldn't afford. In Bergen, I caught
glimpses of another life I could be living. It felt like a world
apart from the one I was currently inhabiting. When I passed
through the tunnel, I moved from the outskirts of my own self
toward the deep parts of it I hadn't yet been able to explore.

My dad watched what would end up being my last professional game. Our team had traveled to Oslo, and we were play-

ing in a large stadium in the city center. Before the game, field managers turned sprinklers on to wet the perfect grass. It was the nicest field I'd ever played on.

In this locker room, our jerseys were hung for us, and our socks and shorts were cleaned, pressed, and folded into a neat pile next to our shin guards. The equipment manager brought our cleats on the plane in a large bag, so we didn't have to worry about packing, and perhaps forgetting, anything essential for the game. I had waited a long time for something to feel professional *enough*. Maybe then, I could rest. In Norway, I was finally playing in a top league. My teammates and I had the accommodations we needed. I had a contributing role on the field. We got paid on time. We flew on planes to our games. Someone did our laundry for us. Someone always refilled the snack bowl. I took a picture of my neatly arranged locker before each game. I had the feeling that I would need proof, the feeling that it was all about to go away.

I remember wanting that last game to fill me up. I wanted us to win, I wanted to score a goal, to have one last celebration. I wanted it to be enough, wanted the sense of an ending, something to write toward. Instead, I limped through the first sixty minutes, slowly tearing an already injured hamstring. I remember running the length of the field to get into the box as a teammate dribbled up the sideline. I knew I only needed one opportunity. I wanted to experience something absolutely appropriate for the occasion.

They tell you to *leave it all on the field*. You leave the bottoms of your cleats, which wear down just a little more each time you play. You leave all of your fluids. You leave so much that, afterward, you need an IV of electrolytes, an injection of saline, a drip of water. You leave the scream of your voice, so you can only speak in a whisper the next day. You leave a surge of adrenaline, endorphins, hormones that make you forget what even happened until you see it on video. You leave bruises on arms; your cleats leave scars in the soft ground. You leave your mind, in a way, and enter into your body without it.

In the middle of *The Waves*, Percival is fighting in a war overseas and makes the ultimate sacrifice: his body, his life. He is named for one of the Knights of the Round Table, an original hero who was on a quest for the Holy Grail. Neville laments: *He is dead. He fell. His horse tripped. He was thrown.* The rest of Percival's story is written through the fogged lens of his friends' grief. *The sails of the world have swung round and caught me on the head. All is over. The lights of the world have gone out. There stands the tree I cannot pass.* He is considered a hero in the book. But he doesn't die a hero's death. Instead, an accident takes his life, a clumsy mistake.

No, I had not gone riding on a horse. I had not been to war, not exactly. I had not died. I had not been mythologized or eulogized. But I had believed, I had tried, I had been consumed by an enormous desire. I had been willing to give up almost anything.

Each sprint was increasingly painful, and, by the sixtieth minute, I was spent, unable to play like myself. I signaled to the coach that I was done. As I walked off the field, I waved up at my dad, who was sitting near the stadium's heights. I remembered the coach from my youth who told me of my potential so *ten years down the road*, I wouldn't wish someone had. It was ten years later now, and I found myself wishing the opposite. I took a seat on the bench and watched my teammates finish off the rest of the game. We won 2–1.

Please let this be over. Then: *I'm not ready for it to be over.*

86'

RECENTLY, I OVERHEARD A STRANGER AT A BASEBALL GAME talking about visualization, the same technique I'd practiced before my soccer games. *The key*, he told his friend, was not vantage point but *perspective*. It was important to view the scene as if from your own eyes. Had I been doing it wrong the whole time? With my eyes closed, I had always watched myself from up above. Like a bird of prey searching for its meal.

87'

VERY FEW VIDEOS EXIST OF ME PLAYING. MOST OF THE FOOT-
age from the internet has been deleted, expired, lost. The DVDs
are becoming scratched, have disappeared in moves, been tossed
away. I do have the one disc still (2007, high school State Championship). I hit play on the video again. I realize the real fear
isn't that I don't know the girl on the screen. The real fear has
something to do with the unflagging focus and devotion I can
see in her face and her movements. I watch as she completes a
pass, moves forward through the defensive line, and takes a shot
that goes wide. What will become of all that desire?

From my dad's house in Portland, where I am sitting now,
I can walk down to my old high school. The building has recently
been demolished, and another one is being built on top of the
soccer field. The new school will be a glassy, modern structure.

My whole life could be divided by fields I have known. So
many of my life's events orbited around their sturdy and terrestrial presence. It was after a practice with Coach Nelson on
a field in downtown Portland, when I was twelve years old, that

I ran up the porch steps to the news of my parents' divorce. It was during a long and quiet drive to the suburban complex where my club team practiced that my eighth-grade boyfriend broke up with me via text message. I spent many driftless days after college graduation on the turf of our school's stadium.

I try to remember a game I played on the field at Lincoln High School, which is now buried under piles of building material and heavy machinery. I try to picture its clean lines, red track, and broken metal stadium seats. But I can only think of the last game I ever played there: senior year, quarterfinals of the state tournament. The rain had been falling for days, and the old field didn't drain properly. We danced around small ponds, the ball stopped here and there to drink. The weather made it impossible to play the game, and we lost 1–0. I wish I could recall a happier memory. I'd like the field to tell me what it saw. But it's under a slab of concrete now and will soon be buried by the towering new building. The specificity of its dimensions and all of its memories will be under layers and layers, will be deep down below the city.

Again, I find myself in the pages of *The Waves*. Bernard, another of Percival's friends, reflects on his passing: *I need silence, and to be alone and to go out, and to save one hour to consider what has happened to my world, what death has done to my world.*

88'

AS MY PLANE FROM NORWAY BEGAN ITS DESCENT INTO THE
United States, I saw green islands scattered across the sea. I
marveled at each tree as it came into view, the solid green mass
soon recognizable as thousands of individual conifers. The scene
reminded me of an article I read years after I left Korea. It was
about the migration path that leads millions of shorebirds to
the Yellow Sea, where they fuel up for their journey from south
to north. The featureless sludge I'd studied from the window
of the conference room had actually been teeming with life. It's
an endangered landscape, gleaming, slick, and precious.

I pressed my face against the plexiglass window of the plane
and saw soccer fields lit up from above, brilliant green squares
announcing themselves over and over again. Four stadium
lights and an unnatural green, ringed by a track pulsing with
activity, even after the streets had gone dark. From up there,
cars looked like ants, houses like boxes, soccer fields like bea-
cons. If there were players on the field, they moved like a school
of minuscule fish on a sea of grass, fluid and relational, involved

in an intricate dance. Each field I have known brings memories back to me, but the ones I don't know still conjure an important feeling. I will always be moved by a pair of lonely goals facing each other along a highway or behind a shuttered school. Their shapes, the outlines, called to me, still call to me now. *We are here, we are still here.*

89'

ONE CRISP NOVEMBER MORNING, ON THE SIDELINES OF A COL-
lege game I'm coaching, I talk to a player who is about to sub
in. I tell her about the other team's formation, I show her where
she needs to go on corner kicks, and I ask her if she's ready. She
says yes, then looks out at the field. Our team is down by two
goals. It is hard to enter a match in the middle, hard to get syn-
chronized with your teammates, hard to understand the flow
of the game, hard to suddenly match its speed. She looks up at
me before she checks in with the sideline referee and asks, *do
you wish you were playing today?*

I know eventually someone will look at me—a friend, a
stranger, a new colleague, a player—and my experience of soccer will be so deep, so broken apart, so forgotten they won't be
able to see it. For now, people often ask me if I miss playing. I
pretend it is a difficult question to answer. I take a moment
before I respond. I might even lie. I miss it every moment of
every day. I will for the rest of my life.

90'

AS I WRITE, I RUN A FINGER OVER THE SCAR ON MY CHEEK. BY
now, it is almost flat. It is a pale pink line, a crease, indistin-
guishable from the wrinkles gathering under my eye.

What has lasted is kept in the closet in the spare bedroom.
There is a cardboard box full of trophies, medals, and other
regalia. It isn't very big, just the size of a milk crate. The collection is a skeleton rather than an archive; years of living out
of a suitcase taught me to constantly evaluate and reduce the
volume of my belongings.

In one of the podcasts I listen to on my commute, Miranda
July talks about a story called "Prizes" by Janet Frame. The
story is, in part, about the narrator's continual dissatisfaction,
her disappointment in the face of her successes. Reflecting on
the story, July remarks, *well, it is very hard to win prizes, to know
what to do with them.*

I sift through the box and unwrap the purple scarf I got
when I played in the Champions League, a trading card with
my face and signature on it from Norway, a gem-encrusted ring

from winning summer league with a team from Seattle. Each time I unpack after moving, I put the box on a shelf and wonder what I'm supposed to do with it. How long should I keep it? Would I be sad if it was lost? I pick up each medal now, feel their hard goldness, wonder if I've spent too much time remembering.

July continues, *I feel like all of the joy is in wanting them and in getting them, but then having them isn't anything.*

90'+

WATCH ANY STRIKER IN THE WANING MINUTES OF A GAME. She'll ask the clock how much time is left. It answers in monotonous pulses: there is still time, there is still time; or: it is nearly over. At the end of regulation, a referee can add *stoppage time*, a subjective allotment of extra minutes that make up for injury or wasted time. The amount of time that passes is inseparable from the immensity of the striker's panic—they are one and the same. With a comfortable lead, ninety minutes have the texture of a single day. Things happen with a calm inevitability. Events are as stable as a sunset, and consequences are modest. Players pass the ball in a sweeping perimeter, slowly and with precision. There is still time to repeat, if they've already done the right thing; to find glory, if glory has thus far proved elusive. Players kick the ball to far corners of the field. They bend over it, trying to protect it and also to injure time to kill the clock.

John Cage once wrote a series of stories called *Indeterminacy*. The length of the compositions varied greatly, but each was supposed to be read aloud over the course of sixty seconds. The readings lengthened time or condensed it, reshaped the vessel of a minute to fit whatever words were recited.

When the striker is losing, she wants to stretch time into a long, thin band, to wring it like a damp towel, to harvest something from it that isn't there anymore. I've been writing these pages for seven years. I must be watching the very last drop fall. Now other players seem to move as if in amber. Time falls away with supernatural ease in big, hulking pieces. This rebellion against natural order can only provoke rage. The striker will throw things, scream at time's nonsense. She will try to reverse the irreversible.

The clock winds down.

ACKNOWLEDGMENTS

In the seven years since I started writing this, I've learned a lot about how many people it takes to bring a book into the world. I owe my gratitude to those who are listed below, and to many more.

I am so thankful that the kind and bright Laura Usselman was my first real advocate. Thank you to Courtney Young and everyone at Riverhead; to Allegra Le Fanu and her team at Bloomsbury; to "the English teachers," Mark Halpern and Jordan Gutlerner, for teaching me how to read like a writer; to the gentle and illuminative Brian Blanchfield; to Jess Arndt, who helped me find structure; to Jim Dawes, who was the first to tell me this writing could be a book; to Abby Waters, my family and collaborator; to Milo Muise and Clare Shearer for their generous and exhaustive editing at every stage; to the editors at *n+1* for being the first to publish some of this writing and for doing it so well. Thank you to my mom, Carey Critchlow, for her fast-twitch muscles and for always being my first reader; to my dad, Brad Cloepfil, for passing with me in the yard and sharing a life of ideas. Thank you especially to Cole Erickson, for living out these dreams with me. And thank you to my teammates who may not know, they are in here.